ROADMAP™ A2+

T0385943

WORKBOOK
with key and online audio

Katy Kelly, Michael Turner

CONTENTS

Vocabulary

Question words

1 **Put the letters in the correct order to make question words.**

1 thwa   _what_
2 rehew   _____
3 chiwh   _____
4 ywh   _____
5 howse   _____
6 newh   _____
7 ohw   _____ / _____

2 **Complete the questions with the words in the box.**

How (x4) ~~What~~ When Where Which
Who Whose

1 _What_ courses do you offer?   _c_
2 _____ much do they cost?   _____
3 _____ long is each class?   _____
4 _____ level is the best for me?   _____
5 _____ many students are in the classes?   _____
6 _____ teaches the class?   _____
7 _____ is the classroom?   _____
8 _____ does the next course start?   _____
9 _____ photo is that?   _____
10 _____ can I pay?   _____

3 **Match answers a–j with questions 1–10 in Exercise 2.**

a They cost £15 per class.
b Your test shows that A2+ is the best level for you.
c We offer General English courses and Business English courses.
d You can pay with cash, credit card or book online.
e There are between 8 and 16 students in each class.
f It's Mr Green's. He's the school manager.
g The next course starts on Monday.
h The teacher's name is Jess. She is very popular.
i Each class is two hours long.
j It's on the first floor. Room 12.

Grammar

Word order in questions

4 **Choose the correct alternatives.**

1 What level *does*/*is* your class?
2 Whose class *do*/*are* you in?
3 What country *does*/*are* you from?
4 Which city *do*/*is* you live in?
5 How long *does*/*is* your journey to school?
6 What kind of transport *do*/*are* you take?
7 Who *do*/*is* your favourite singer?
8 Why *do*/*are* you want to learn English?

5 **Correct the mistake in each question.**

      What is your
1 ⁄ ~~Your~~ favourite food, ~~what is~~?

2 How many hours you spend online?

3 Are you like reading?

4 Where you go at weekends?

5 You talk to your friends online?

6 Where your favourite restaurant?

7 From where are you?

8 What book your favourite is?

9 You live in a city?

10 Do you interested in sports?

6 **Complete the questions with two words. Use the prsent simple.**

1 A: I really like rock music.
   B: Me too! Who _is your_ favourite band?
   A: I love The Killers.
2 A: I can speak four different languages: Italian, German, English and Chinese.
   B: Really? _____ write in Chinese?
   A: Yes, but it's really difficult to learn.
3 A: Do you want to go out tonight after work?
   B: Yes, I do! What time _____ finish work?
   A: I finish at 6 p.m. Let's meet at 8 p.m. in town.
4 A: I'm afraid of cats.
   B: Really? Why _____ afraid of cats?
   A: I don't know! I just don't like them.
5 A: My journey to school takes a long time.
   B: Really? How long _____ take?
   A: Nearly 90 minutes! I need to take three buses!

Vocabulary

Success

1 **Complete the phrases with the verbs in the box.**

ask   have   listen   plan   start
take (x2)   try

1 .... a lot of questions
2 .... carefully
3 .... care of yourself
4 .... again
5 .... clear goals
6 .... new things
7 .... your time well
8 .... time off

2 **Choose the correct alternatives.**

1 *Listen/Ask* carefully to other people. They can help you!
2 It's really important to *have/do* clear goals.
3 It's also important to *plan/take* your time well.
4 Remember that if you make a mistake, you can start *another/again*.
5 Remember to take *care/careful* of yourself – eat good food and get lots of sleep.
6 Take time *off/out* work. It's important not to work too hard.
7 Don't always do the same things. It's good to *have/try* new things, too!
8 It's useful to *ask/say* a lot of questions when you learn something new.

Grammar

Expressions of frequency

3 **Complete the sentences with the words in the box.**

all   always   every   hardly   often   once   rarely   week

1 I usually do exercise .... a day.
2 I .... arrive early to class. I don't like to be late.
3 She checks her email .... the time!
4 I want to pass my exam, so I study .... day after college.
5 I like going out, so I .... stay at home on Friday evenings.
6 I don't .... watch sport on TV – I think it's boring!
7 I visit my mum once a ...., usually on Saturdays.
8 My best friend lives in another town, so I .... ever see her.

4 **Put the words in the correct order to make sentences.**

1 I'm / on / always / time
I'm always on time.
2 I / late / Fridays / often / work / on
....
3 He's / after / usually / class / tired
....
4 I / night / go / running / never / at
....
5 doesn't / She / emails / usually / weekends / check / her / at
....
6 I / the / all / time / go / there
....
7 I / to / relax / have / rarely / time
....
8 the / to / I / hardly / cinema / ever / go
....

5 **Complete the second sentence so the meaning is the same as the first sentence. Use the words in the box.**

always   every month   never   often   once a week   rarely   ~~usually~~

1 It's a very busy job and I normally have a lot of work to do.
It's a very busy job and I *usually have a lot of work to do* .
2 My job is really fun, so I hardly ever get bored.
My job is really fun, so I'm ....
3 My students make me happy all the time!
My students ....
4 I have a team meeting every Monday.
I have ....
5 We get paid on the last Friday of the month.
We get paid ....
6 I don't ever have enough sleep!
I ....
7 I work late two or three times a week.
I ....

1c

Grammar

Present simple and present continuous

1 **Choose the correct alternatives.**
  1 a I *study/'m studying* English a lot these days.
    b I *study/'m studying* English twice a week.
  2 a I *try/'m trying* to stay healthy. It's important.
    b I *try/'m trying* yoga at the moment. It's great.
  3 a I *usually take/'m taking* a taxi today. I'm really late!
    b I *usually take/'m taking* the train to work. It's cheap and easy.
  4 a I *use/'m using* a laptop when I'm in the office.
    b I *use/'m using* a laptop at the moment. I'm in a café.
  5 a I *talk/'m talking* to my best friend right now on social media. She needs my advice.
    b I *talk/'m talking* to my best friend every day. We're very close.
  6 a I *cook/'m cooking* for myself most days. I enjoy it.
    b I *cook/'m cooking* a curry. Would you like to join us?

2 **Decide if the underlined words in each sentence are correct (✓) or incorrect (✗). Then correct the incorrect words.**

    I usually wake
  1 / ~~I'm usually waking~~ up at 6 a.m. on weekdays. ✗

  2 I have a shower every morning.

  3 I can't speak now, I cook dinner!

  4 I work for a big company in the city.

  5 She's cleaning the house at the moment.

  6 I'm from Italy, but this year I live in Spain.

  7 She tries a new lifestyle this month.

3 **Complete the conversations with the present simple or present continuous form of the verbs in brackets.**
  1 **A:** Why _____*are you crying*_____ (you/cry)?
    B: I'm watching a really sad film on my laptop.
  2 **A:** What _____ (you/do)?
    B: I'm an architect.
  3 **A:** Do you want to go out for some lunch?
    B: Sorry. I can't. _____ (I/work) on a presentation right now.
  4 **A:** Where is Mark? He usually works here on Fridays.
    B: Yes, but _____ (he/visit) his brother in America at the moment.
  5 **A:** Is that Gloria's car?
    B: No. _____ (she/drive) a sports car.
  6 **A:** That smells great! What _____ (you/cook)?
    B: It's spaghetti bolognese.
  7 **A:** What kind of exercise do you do?
    B: _____ (I/try) a new Pilates class at the moment.

Vocabulary

Everyday activities

4 **Cross out the word that does not go with the verb in bold.**
  1 **get** up/~~family~~/dressed
  2 **watch** a film/cards/a show
  3 **take** a break/a picture/the answers
  4 **start/finish** money/school/ a language course
  5 **play** video games/tennis/social media
  6 **spend time with** friends/email/family
  7 **have** a language course/lunch/ a good time
  8 **check** social media/school/the answers

5 **Complete the schedule with the phrases in the box.**

~~have a shower~~   have lunch
spend time with family   start work
take a break   watch a film

6.00	get up early.
6.10	**1** *have a shower*
6.30	have breakfast
7.30	go to work
8.30	**2** _____
8.35	check emails
11.00	**3** _____
11.05	check social media
13.00	**4** _____
17.00	finish work
18.00	get home
18.30	**5** _____
19.00	have dinner
20.00	**6** _____
23.00	go to bed

1D

Functional language

Ask for and check information

1 Complete the sentences with the words in the box.

> clear get help need (x2) one repeat this

1 **A:** Excuse me. Can you _____ me? What bus do I need to get to the train station?
   B: Yeah, sure. You _____ to take bus number 5.
2 **A:** Please write your name at the top of the page. Is that _____?
   B: Sorry, where? Can you _____ that, please?
3 **A:** Here's the letter for the school trip.
   B: What do I _____ to do with it now?
   A: Your parents must sign it, then bring it back to me. Did you _____ that?
4 **A:** There are two books with the same name here. Which _____ is it?
   B: Oh right, sorry! It's _____ one here with the blue cover.

2 Choose the correct alternatives.

1 There are two people in the class with the name Maria. *Which/Who* one is the singer?
2 This is difficult. *Do/Can* you help me?
3 *What/Who* do I need to do in this activity?
4 Please don't write on the exam paper. *Do/Is* that clear?
5 To find the coffee shop, you need *to/are* turn right after the station.
6 I can't hear you. *Do/Can* you repeat that, please?
7 Remember to answer all the questions. *Are/Did* you get that?
8 No, not that one. *It's/Is* this one here!

3 Match the sentence halves.

1 Excuse me. Can you   *d*
2 The house we've bought is this   _____
3 Which street   _____
4 You must switch off your phones. Is that   _____
5 I've finished. What do I   _____
6 When you finish, you   _____
7 I can't hear you. Can you   _____
8 Make sure you sign every page. Did you   _____

a repeat that, please?
b is it?
c need to put up your hand.
d help me, please? I'm lost.
e get that?
f clear?
g one here, next to the old railway bridge.
h need to do next?

1

Listening

1 🔊 **1.01 Listen to part of a radio programme. What's it about?**
a different languages
b different greetings in English
c greetings that are bad to use in English.

2 **Listen again. Number the countries in the order you hear them (1–4).**
a Ireland _____
b Australia _____
c Scotland _____
d the US _____

3a **Are the sentences true (T) or false (F)?**
1 There are many different ways to say hello and goodbye in English. _____
2 In Australia, people say hi and bye in different ways. _____
3 In Australia, people say *Cheerio* to say hello. _____
4 In the US, people say *Take it easy* to say goodbye. _____
5 In Ireland, people say *Hey! What's up?* or *What's happening?* _____
6 In Ireland, people often leave without saying goodbye. _____
7 In Scotland, you can say *See you after* for goodbye. _____
8 Jack says that Irish greetings are his favourite. _____

b **Listen again and check.**

4 **Read the extracts from the recording. Match the words in bold with the meanings a–e.**
1 I'd like to **introduce** Jack Tunnel. _____
2 an English language **expert** _____
3 Australia has some interesting **greetings**. _____
4 They sound so **friendly**! _____
5 There you have it, **listeners**! _____

a things you say when you meet people
b helpful and nice to someone
c someone who knows a lot about a subject
d people who listen to the radio
e tell someone another person's name

Reading

1 Read the magazine article. Who does the writer want to find out about?

   a old people

   b boring people

   c interesting people

2 Read the article again. Are the sentences true (T) or false (F)?

   1 The writer is spending a week with Valerie. ....

   2 Valerie wants to be 108 years old. ....

   3 Valerie eats eggs which are not cooked. ....

   4 Valerie goes to sleep after breakfast. ....

   5 Valerie always eats the same food for lunch. ....

   6 Dinner is a simple meal. ....

   7 Valerie doesn't always write in her diary in the evening. ....

   8 The article says that you should not try Valerie's routine. ....

3 Read the article again. Choose the correct alternatives.

   1 Valerie's bedtime is *different/the same* every night.

   2 Valerie *sometimes/always* sleeps well.

   3 Her daily routine is *easy/difficult* to follow.

   4 Valerie gets up *early/late* in the morning.

   5 Valerie says that the sun makes her *happy/unhappy*.

   6 She *rarely/often* misses doing exercise.

   7 Valerie and her friends *never/sometimes* watch TV together.

   8 Valerie *rarely/always* has a nap after lunch.

   9 *Every day/Some days,* she writes in her diary.

4 Match the words in the box with definitions 1–6.

boiled diary nap raw secret unusual

   1 cooked in hot water ....

   2 a short sleep in the day time ....

   3 not cooked ....

   4 different, not normal ....

   5 a book to write about things you do and how you feel ....

   6 something which only you or a few people know ....

A day in the life of …

Valerie Ackerman

As part of our series A day in the life of …, we are spending a day with unusual, exciting and special people to find out about how they live.

Today, I'm spending time with Valerie Susan Ackerman. Valerie is 108 years old and I'm going to live a day in her life and find out about her daily routines and habits.

We start the day at 7.00 in the morning.

'I always get up with the sun,' says Valerie. 'I never miss the morning sunshine. It makes me happy all day!'

This early morning habit is just one example in Valerie's day that she says helps her live a long and happy life.

For breakfast, Valerie and I eat two raw eggs mixed with olive oil and we drink a cup of hot water with lemon. I like eggs in the morning, but I prefer them cooked!

Next, it's exercise time. Every day, Valerie walks around the village square five times, without taking any rest.

'Sometimes when it's cold or raining, it can be difficult,' says Valerie, 'but I hardly ever miss this exercise. I think it's a very important part of my day!'

After her exercise routine, Valerie meets up with her friends. Together they listen to music, read poetry and play games. 'We don't watch TV. It makes us very tired and we don't think it's fun.'

Valerie laughs and jokes with her friends and then goes home for lunch. She eats boiled corn and fish and drinks a big cup of hot chocolate. For 70 years, Valerie has eaten the same for lunch – always corn and always fish.

'It's the hot chocolate I love!' says Valerie.

After lunch, it's time for a nap. Sleeping for two hours in the afternoon keeps Valerie relaxed and ready for the evening. Sixty years of napping every day – that sounds good to me! In the evening, we make a simple dinner of cheese and bread. Then Valerie sits down to write in her diary. She has over 100 diaries because each evening she always writes down her thoughts and feelings.

'It helps to clear my mind and finish the day,' says Valerie, 'and then my mind is free to start again the next day!'

Then at eleven o'clock, it's time for bed. Valerie sleeps for eight hours every night. She says she always sleeps well and never has bad dreams.

Now we know how to live to be a hundred years old! Valerie's habits and routines are fun and really easy. Why not try them?

Writing

1 **Read the blog and choose the best title a, b or c.**

   a Raul's work habits

   b Raul's study habits

   c Raul's free-time habits

A lot of my friends ask me how I do so well in my exams, so I thought I'd share my top tips on how to be a successful student.

1 Time of day

I work 12–8 p.m. in a hotel, so I usually feel tired in the evenings. That's why I study in the morning.

2 Writing notes

I write study notes so that I can remember what I read. I forget things easily, so it helps me to write everything in a notebook.

3 A special place to study

I usually sit near a window because of the light. I need a table and a comfortable chair but nothing else!

4 Eating the right food

It's important to eat good food because it helps me to concentrate. When I study, I usually eat nuts and bananas.

5 Music and TV

Sometimes I like listening to music when I read my study notes. I can't watch TV when I study because I find it difficult to do two things at the same time.

6 Take breaks

I think that it is a good idea to take a short break and move around every two hours. I like to have a 15-minute break and walk around the garden or the house.

2 **Choose the correct alternatives.**

   1 Raul usually feels tired in the *morning/evening*.

   2 He finds it *easy/difficult* to remember things.

   3 He *writes/doesn't write* notes to help him.

   4 He needs a comfortable *window/chair* to help him study.

   5 He *likes/doesn't like* to eat when he studies.

   6 He says that TV *helps/doesn't help* him study.

   7 When he studies, he *takes/doesn't take* a break every two hours.

   8 He likes to *sleep/exercise* during his short break.

3 **Read the Focus box. Then complete sentences 1–6 below with *that's why, because (of)* or *so that*.**

Explaining reasons and results

Use *because (of)* and *so that* to give reasons.

*It's important to eat good food **because** it helps me to concentrate.*

*I usually study near a window **because of the light**.*

*I write study notes **so that** I can remember what I read.*

Use *that's why* to explain a result.

*I usually feel tired in the evenings. **That's why** I study in the morning.*

---

   1 It usually rains here in January. _____ I take my umbrella everywhere I go.

   2 I eat healthy food _____ I can concentrate well.

   3 Hannah usually does her homework in the evening _____ she has the weekend free.

   4 I walk to work _____ there is a lot of traffic in the mornings.

   5 The trains are all late today _____ the bad weather.

   6 Marina is going to work in America. _____ she's learning English.

Prepare

4 **You're going to write a blog about your own study habits. Look at the headings in Raul's blog and make notes for each one.**

Write

5 **Write your blog, including the six headings. Use your notes in Exercise 4 and the Focus box to help you.**

Vocabulary

Feelings

1 **Complete the sentences with the adjectives in the box.**

afraid   angry   bored   excited
~~happy~~   nervous   relaxed   stressed
surprised   worried

1 My sister was very ___*happy*___ when she finished her exams.
2 Children are often _____ of the dark.
3 Jen is _____ about her interview tomorrow.
4 Susan is feeling _____ and needs a holiday!
5 Betty is really _____ about her birthday party on Saturday.
6 I'm really _____ that Jim isn't helping me cook dinner.
7 I'm _____ in my job, so I want to find a new one.
8 I enjoy spending time with Philip because he's a very _____ person.
9 Kim is _____ about the project because there are some problems.
10 My sister was _____ to see me at the airport.

2 **Choose the correct alternatives.**

1 A: What's wrong? You look really *relaxed/angry*!
   B: Yes, I am. My boss said she isn't *happy/bored* with my work.
2 A: Are you *worried/bored* about your interview tomorrow?
   B: No, not really. I feel quite *relaxed/afraid* because I know a lot about the job.
3 A: I'm not going to tonight's yoga class. I'm a bit *surprised/bored* with it.
   B: Really? Yoga really helps me when I'm feeling *excited/stressed*.
4 A: I'm so *excited/afraid* about going to Italy this summer.
   B: Aren't you *bored/nervous* about going on your own?
5 A: I'm really *bored/excited*, there's nothing to do here.
   B: I'm *surprised/angry* to hear that. I think it's great!

Grammar

Past simple

3 **Complete the sentences with the past simple form of the verbs in brackets.**

1 Sebastian _____ (go) to visit his family in Hong Kong.
2 We _____ (decide) to visit the nature park and not the zoo.
3 Ruth _____ (try) to help her sister with her homework.
4 They _____ (show) us around their beautiful new home.
5 Hugo _____ (feel) really tired and went home early.
6 We _____ (talk) about which present to buy Carly.
7 They _____ (go) to Cape Town this morning.
8 Phil and Ben _____ (be) happy to help me fix my car.
9 Robin _____ (watch) the football match with his friends.
10 I _____ (be) surprised to see some new students in the class.

4 **Choose the correct alternatives.**

1 Hilda *walk/walked* to the swimming pool with her daughter.
2 James *crying/cried* at the end of the film because it was very sad.
3 We *was/were* really cold on the train because there was no heating.
4 Before I *had/have* a baby, I had more time to read books.
5 The waiter *write/wrote* down the order in his notebook.
6 Rachel *flying/flew* to Japan yesterday.
7 I *see/saw* my old teacher in town on Saturday.
8 Georgia *was/were* very lucky to get the job.

5 **Complete the text with the past simple form of the verbs in the box.**

arrive   be (x2)   decide   feel   fly   look   show   talk   try
visit   watch

In my job I don't get many holidays. I'm always too busy with work!
So this year, I ¹_____ to take a holiday in the sun with my family.
We ²_____ very excited and ³_____ at the airport early. We
had to check in for the flight and hand in our luggage. As we queued,
we ⁴_____ about all the things we wanted to do on holiday. When
it was our turn to check in, I ⁵_____ at the tickets. I realised that
I had booked the wrong holiday. Our tickets were for two weeks' holiday
in Manchester, not Morocco! We ⁶_____ to change the tickets, but
it wasn't possible. I ⁷_____ my hotel booking to the travel company,
but they couldn't change it. We were so angry! In the end, we
⁸_____ to Manchester. The holiday ⁹_____ a lot of fun.
I ¹⁰_____ relaxed and happy. We ¹¹_____ films and
¹²_____ great museums. We were surprised to have such a good
holiday so close to home!

Vocabulary

Past time expressions

1 **Choose the correct alternatives.**

1 We visited China *at/in* 2014 and saw the Great Wall.

2 Did you go to Brian's 30th birthday party *last/until* August?

3 *When/As* I was ten, I went to live with my aunt in Switzerland.

4 Pete came to visit us two weeks *until/ago*.

5 We moved house *on/at* 17th March.

6 Bob stayed in the job *until/when* 2017 and then started his own business.

2 **Match the sentence halves.**

1 We didn't know each other until last ___*d*___

2 They had a summer holiday in Cuba in ___

3 We met my brother's new girlfriend at a party three weeks ___

4 Sally learnt German when she was ___

5 Gemma didn't have her own car until ___

6 We got married on ___

a seven years old.

b 2016.

c this year.

d February.

e 17th August.

f ago.

3 **Complete the sentences with the words in the box.**

> ago (x2)   in   last   on (x2)   until   when

1 I started playing tennis _____ I was about 12 years old.

2 I saw that new film at the cinema a week _____ .

3 We met _____ January this year on a skiing holiday.

4 _____ year, three new hotels opened in our town.

5 Daniel lived in France _____ last year, when he moved to Germany.

6 We went to Paris _____ my birthday.

7 I always meet Claire for coffee _____ Saturdays.

8 I met my best friend 15 years _____ .

Grammar

Past simple negative and questions

4 **Choose the correct alternatives.**

1 Last week I *don't/didn't* go out so that I could study.

2 We *weren't/wasn't* surprised that the flight was delayed.

3 Why *did/was* Susan so stressed yesterday evening?

4 Liv *wasn't/didn't* know how to use the new computer system at work.

5 I *wasn't/didn't* excited about the project.

6 I tried to help her, but she *didn't/wasn't* listen to me.

7 Greg *wasn't/weren't* good at sports at school.

8 What *did/was* you say to him?

5 **Complete the text with the past simple form of the verbs in brackets.**

When I [1] _____ (be) 18 years old, I [2] _____ (go) backpacking across Europe with all my friends from school. We [3] _____ (not have) a lot of money, but we [4] _____ (have) a wonderful time. We [5] _____ (try) to plan the trip well, but there [6] _____ (be) a few surprises! We [7] _____ (not find) many cheap places to stay, and in the second week of our trip, my friend Becky [8] _____ (fall over) and hurt her knee. But it was fun. We [9] _____ (eat) a lot of great food and [10] _____ (laugh) a lot, too!

6 **Put the words in the correct order to make questions.**

1 Jim / this / When / morning / did / arrive?

2 buy / your / you / Where / bike / did?

3 at / Who / party / Shona's / was?

4 you / on / go / Where / holiday / did?

5 late / was / this / Why / Billy / morning?

6 finish / What / they / did / work / time?

7 Why / she / to / travel / Italy / did?

8 see / Which / at / you / did / cinema / film / the?

2c

Vocabulary

Adjectives to describe food

1 **Complete the sentences with the adjectives in the box. Sometimes more than one answer might be possible.**

creamy   delicious   dry   fresh   hot   light   plain
sour   sweet

1 This drink has a lot of lemons, so it's a bit _____ .
2 Can you make a _____ sauce for the pasta?
3 I usually cook with _____ ingredients.
4 I didn't enjoy the roast lamb because it was too

_____ .

5 I often eat a _____ salad at lunchtime.
6 My friend likes _____ food, which isn't very tasty.
7 Careful! That dish is really _____ .
8 I always eat something _____ after dinner.
9 This cake is _____ . Can I have the recipe?

2 **Choose the correct alternatives.**

1 This coffee isn't very *hot/dry*. Can I have another one?
2 My children only want to eat *sour/sweet* things, like cakes and doughnuts.
3 This salad is *light/sweet* and quick to make.
4 Those cakes look *dry/delicious*, but they don't taste very good.
5 When you don't feel well, it can be helpful to eat *plain/light* toast.
6 I think I baked the biscuits for too long. They are very *dry/sour*.
7 The vegetables at this supermarket don't look very *sweet/fresh*.
8 I love French cheeses which are very *creamy/hot*.
9 Sweet and *sour/fresh* is a common taste in Chinese cooking.

Grammar

Quantifiers

3 **Match the sentence halves.**

1 Let's grow lots of ___*b*___
2 To make sandwiches we need some _____
3 There's a _____
4 Did you buy an _____
5 I need to buy a few _____
6 Add a little _____
7 There aren't any _____
8 There's only a bit of _____

a fish pie in the oven.
b fresh herbs in our garden.
c coffee left in the pot.
d onion at the shop?
e fresh bread.
f hot sauce to make it tasty.
g eggs so that I can make an omelette.
h dishes I don't like to eat.

4 **Choose the correct alternatives.**

A: Hi, Matt. How are you?
B: Hey, Raul. I really need [1]*a/some* help. I want to cook something delicious tonight.
A: How about paella?
B: That's a good idea. I'll need [2]*a few/a lot of* rice and [3]*some/an* onions. Is that right?
A: Yes. You also need [4]*lots of/a* seafood.
B: How about [5]*a/an* lobster, [6]*a little/a few* tiger prawns and [7]*a lot/some* mussels?
A: Great! Also add [8]*some/a little* vegetables and [9]*a/a few* herbs and spices. Which herbs have you got in your cupboard?
B: Let's see. There's [10]*any/a little* parsley and [11]*a lot/a few* of thyme.
A: OK. You also need [12]*a few/a little* cloves of garlic and [13]*a/an* lemon. Oh, and something which is very important – [14]*not any/some* saffron.
B: Thanks a lot for your help, Matt!

5 **Complete the sentences with the words in the box.**

a   a lot   an   any   bit   little   of   some

1 Please add a _____ of sugar to my tea.
2 There's only a _____ cheese but there's lots of ham.
3 There's _____ coconut milk in the curry but not a lot.
4 I always have lots _____ chocolate sauce on my ice cream.
5 You need to add _____ of water.
6 I drink _____ glass of orange juice every day.
7 There isn't _____ salt in this dish.
8 I eat _____ apple every day.

Functional language

Show interest and excitement

1 Complete the phrases with the words in the box.

exciting   guess   lovely   next   sounds   that's
way   where

1 _____ amazing!
2 _____ what happened to me!?
3 How _____!
4 Guess _____ I went?
5 That _____ wonderful!
6 Thank you, they're _____ .
7 No _____!
8 What happened _____ ?

2 Match sentences 1–6 with responses a–f.

1 I passed my driving test. _____
2 I'm graduating from university next week. _____
3 I've cooked lasagne for dinner. _____
4 I want to start Pilates classes. _____
5 My mum bought me a laptop for my birthday. _____
6 I had an interview for a new job yesterday. _____

a That's great. You worked really hard this year.
b Brilliant! Now you can drive us to the beach!
c What a good idea! Can I come?
d No way! You're so lucky!
e Really? How did it go?
f That sounds delicious. I can't wait!

3 Choose the correct alternatives.

A: Guess ¹*where/what* I went yesterday! On a date!
B: ²*How/That* exciting! ³*What/Who* did you go with?
A: Carlos!
B: Carlos from your office!? ⁴*No way/Not away*!
A: Yes!
B: ⁵*How/What* did that go?
A: Great! It was so romantic. He took me to his favourite restaurant.
B: That ⁶*sounds/how* lovely! ⁷*What/Who* happened next?
A: We went for a coffee and we talked for hours.
B: ⁸*That's/What's* great. I'm so happy for you!

Listening

1 🔊 **2.01** Listen to a chef talking about traditional English food. Match dishes 1–3 with descriptions A–C.

1 bubble and squeak _____   2 beef pasties _____

3 Eccles cakes _____

2 Listen again. Are the sentences true (T) or false (F)?

1 You usually eat beef pasties with a knife and fork. _____
2 Pasties are popular in the winter. _____
3 You can only buy pasties in bakeries. _____
4 The speaker's grandmother made him bubble and squeak when he was young. _____
5 You make bubble and squeak with fresh meat and vegetables. _____
6 The name 'bubble and squeak' comes from the noise it makes when you cook it. _____
7 The Eccles cake recipe is 300 years old. _____
8 Eccles cakes usually have apples inside. _____

3a Choose the correct option a, b or c.

1 The vegetables in a beef pasty are usually ...
   a mushrooms, onions and peas.
   b potatoes, onions and carrots.
   c peas, onions and carrots.
2 People first made beef pasties ...
   a 200 years ago.   b 300 years ago.
   c 400 years ago.
3 Most people like to eat beef pasties with ...
   a salt and pepper.   b sugar.   c ketchup.
4 The speaker says that bubble and squeak ...
   a looks bad but tastes good.
   b looks good and tastes good.
   c looks good but tastes bad.
5 If you want to try bubble and squeak, ...
   a you can buy it in a restaurant.
   b you need to cook it yourself.
   c you can buy it in the supermarket.
6 Eccles cakes come from ...
   a Liverpool.   b Cornwall.   c Manchester.
7 Eccles cakes are ...
   a expensive.   b healthy.   c unhealthy.
8 The best place to try an Eccles cake is ...
   a at a bakery.   b at a supermarket.   c at home.

b Listen again and check.

Reading

1 Read the article about stories from the past. Which parts of the world do these come from?

1 fables ....
2 hula ....
3 griots ....
4 cave art ....

2 Read the article again. Choose the correct alternatives.

1 A long time ago, fables *were/weren't* written in books.
2 These days, people *read/don't read* fables.
3 *Men/Women* usually danced the hula.
4 The dancers *chanted/played drums*.
5 A griot *has/doesn't have* a good memory.
6 A griot *has to/doesn't have to* learn how to play a kora.
7 Sixty thousand years ago in Spain, people *used/didn't use* caves to tell stories.
8 *A few/A lot of* the paintings show animals.

3 Read the article again and answer the questions.

1 Why did Greek people listen to fables?
....

2 Who was a famous Greek storyteller?
....

3 What colour were the hula clothes?
....

4 Why were hula stories important?
....

5 What does a griot do?
....

6 Why does it take many years to become a griot?
....

7 In Spain, where can we find the paintings in the caves?
....

8 When did people make the cave paintings?
....

4 Match the words in bold in the article with meanings 1–5.

1 more important than usual things
....

2 a hole under the ground ....
3 very old ....
4 almost the same as something else
....

5 things people do wrong ....

Stories from the past

Stories are very important to us. We all love stories. Today, we tell stories in books, music, photos, art and films, but in the past we told stories in a different way. This article looks at four ways of telling stories that are older than books!

Fables: a spoken story

Long before we wrote stories on paper and in books, people told each other stories and they remembered the stories. The stories were called fables and were popular in Greece a long time ago. Fables were traditional stories that taught lessons about things people should do. They helped people live good lives. People listened to the stories and learnt lessons from other people's **mistakes**. One of the most famous storytellers was called Aesop. People still read and tell his stories today.

Hula: a dance story

The people who lived in Hawaii a long time ago did not write. They danced to share their stories. The dance was called 'hula' and was usually performed by men. People played drums and the men danced hula and chanted. The dancers wore dark green clothes made from plants and trees. The hula stories were **special** because they told the history of the Hawaiian people.

Griots: a song story

In West Africa, there are special storytellers called 'griots'. A griot tells the story of their village. Griots have very good memories. They remember the name of everyone who lives and dies in the village. They sing their stories to music and they play a kora. A kora is **similar** to a guitar. It takes many years to become a griot. This is because a griot has to learn a lot of information.

Cave art: a painted story

People told stories to one another before we spoke languages! In Spain, there are **ancient** paintings on the walls of caves. These paintings are 60,000 years old! We don't know the meaning of these cave paintings, but many of them show animals. Some people believe that a long time ago the paintings helped people to share important information with one another. These **cave** paintings could be the oldest stories in the world!

Writing

1 **Read the blog post. What's it about?**
- a a difficult journey
- b a difficult day at the office
- c a difficult presentation

What a day!

Have you had a really good day or a really bad day? Tell us here!

A month ago, I had a very bad day. It was the morning of my big presentation at work and I really wanted it to be successful.

The day started well. I woke up early, took a shower and had a good breakfast. I carefully checked my presentation one last time. I was happy with it, so I put my notes in my bag and calmly left the house. I felt great!

On my way to the bus stop, I looked for my wallet, but it wasn't there. I quickly looked in my pockets. Nothing! I went back to my house and then realised that I didn't have my house keys either. 'No!' I shouted angrily, but it was too late. My wallet and my keys were inside the house!

Disaster! I had no money for the bus and my presentation was at 9 a.m. What to do? I found my bicycle at the side of the house, so I cycled fast to get to work. It took me nearly an hour and halfway there it started to rain.

When I arrived at work, I was tired and wet, and I felt terrible. I walked slowly up the stairs and into the office. My boss laughed loudly when he saw me. 'What happened to you?' he asked.

'It's a long story,' I answered.

'I hope you look better tomorrow when you have your big presentation,' he said!

2 **Read the blog post again. Put events a–j in the correct order.**
- a get bike ......
- b get to work ......
- c look in pockets ......
- d can't find wallet ......
- e get wet ......
- f can't find keys ......
- g have breakfast ......
- h leave house ......
- i check presentation ......
- j take a shower ___1___

3a **Read the Focus box. Then underline the adverbs in the blog post.**

Using adverbs to describe actions

Use adverbs like *angrily*, *calmly*, *quickly* and *slowly* to describe how an action happens. They help the reader imagine the events in a story more clearly.

Adverbs are usually formed by adding -*ly* to the end of adjectives.

I **quickly looked** in my pockets.

They can come before or after the verb.

I **carefully checked** my presentation.

I **walked slowly** up the stairs.

Some adjectives have irregular adverbs.

fast (adjective) – *fast* (adverb)

good (adjective) – *well* (adverb)

b **Complete the sentences with the adverbs in the box.**

> badly   ~~carefully~~   easily   happily   quickly   quietly
> slowly   well

1 I _carefully_ picked up the baby.
2 The day started .... and then got even worse!
3 I .... ate my food and ran out of the house.
4 The children laughed .... in the garden.
5 I .... closed the door because I didn't want to wake my parents up.
6 I was prepared, so I passed the test ....
7 I walked .... because I was really tired.
8 We played .... and won the match.

Prepare

4a **You're going to write a blog post about a good or bad day. It can be real or imaginary. First, make notes about the questions below.**
- When did it happen?
- Where did it happen?
- Who was there?
- What happened before?
- What happened in the end?
- Why was it good/bad?
- How did you feel?
- How did other people feel?

b **Write down any verbs and adverbs you can use in your story.**

Write

5 **Write your blog post. Use your notes in Exercise 4 and the blog post in Exercise 1 to help you.**

Vocabulary

Adjectives to describe places

1 **Choose the correct alternatives.**

1 I don't like this part of the city. There's a lot of rubbish and the streets aren't very *clean*/*beautiful*.

2 The guided tour we went on was really *lively*/*interesting*. We learnt a lot about the area.

3 There are so many people in the museum today – it's really *modern*/*crowded*!

4 I had a great holiday in Ibiza, but it wasn't very *dirty*/*cheap* – it cost a lot of money!

5 The park near my flat isn't near any roads, so it's nice and *noisy*/*peaceful*.

6 There's so much to do in Madrid. It's an *exciting*/*old* place to visit.

2 **Complete the text with the words in the box.**

> beautiful   dirty   interesting   lively
> modern   noisy   old   popular

The town I live in is called Amira. It's very
¹_____, more than 2,000 years, in fact! I've
lived here for ten years now. It's a very ²_____
place, with lots of people and noise. There's a mix of
old and ³_____ buildings and there are many
⁴_____ tourist sites which everybody likes to
visit during the summer. There's also a ⁵_____
beach close to the centre where you can relax.
There are lots of festivals in spring time, with music
and dancing, so it's quite ⁶_____ at that time
of year. The big parties in the city centre make the
streets very ⁷_____ – there's so much rubbish!
But it's only for a short time, so it's not really a
problem. I think everyone should come and visit my
town. It's ⁸_____ because there are so many
things to do, and the sun always shines!

Grammar

Comparatives

3 **Put the words in the correct order to make sentences.**

1 to phone friends / it's easier / than to write emails
   It's easier to phone friends than to write emails.

2 than English / maths / is more difficult / my sister thinks
   _____

3 than riding a bike / is worse for the environment / driving a car
   _____

4 is less boring / working with other people / than working alone / I think
   _____

5 they say that / than the old theatre / is uglier / the new theatre
   _____

6 than it was before / is cleaner now / the river
   _____

7 as / is not / this class / as easy / the last class
   _____

8 your city / weather / has better / than mine
   _____

9 faster than / Brigit doesn't run / her sister
   _____

10 than my laptop / my mobile was / less expensive
    _____

4 **Complete the sentences with the comparative form of the adjectives in brackets.**

1 The street is _____ (noisy) now because of the new student houses. There's a party every night of the week!

2 This area is _____ (beautiful) and _____ (peaceful) than the centre of town. Listen how quiet it is!

3 Homes in cities are often _____ (not big) homes in villages.

4 I think that small towns are _____ (good) places to live in than big cities.

5 Walking home alone late at night is _____ (safe) than walking home late at night with other people.

6 Cities with cheap public transport can be _____ (popular) than cities with expensive buses and trains.

7 This area is _____ (old) than the area where I live.

8 The gym is _____ (busy) during the week than at the weekend. It's crowded at weekends!

9 My old home was _____ (not modern) my new home.

10 This city is _____ (interesting) to visit in summer than in winter.

Vocabulary

Hotels and places to stay

1 **Choose the correct alternatives.**

1 There's a *24-hour/four-star* reception, so you can call us if you need anything.

2 The website said that every room has a *free parking/sea view*.

3 I'm tired tonight. Let's get room *service/transfer* and eat here.

4 There isn't any *organised/free* parking, so we need to pay extra for our car.

5 There isn't an airport *transfer/tour*, so we'll have to get a taxi.

6 Your room rate has breakfast *included/out*.

7 We stayed in a *double/star* room, but it was very small!

8 My mum loves organised *tours/transfers*, but I hate doing activities in big groups.

2 **Complete the sentences with the words in the box.**

> included   organised   out   parking
> reception   service   star   view

1 We arrived very late, so we ordered room _____ .

2 We ate a lot every morning because breakfast was _____ .

3 Oh wow, look at the lovely sea _____ from our window!

4 We're going to hire a car – is there free _____ ?

5 It's a four-_____ hotel: it's got a swimming pool and really good restaurant!

6 Check _____ is at 10 a.m. tomorrow, so don't sleep too late!

7 Shall we go on an _____ tour to the capital city tomorrow?

8 There's a 24-hour _____ , so you can arrive at any time.

Grammar

Superlatives

3 **Choose the correct alternatives.**

1 The *most/more* exciting thing on holiday was when we saw the elephants.

2 We climbed *the highest/highest* mountain on the island.

3 That was the *least/less* interesting film of them all!

4 I think the *most cheap/cheapest* option is to go camping.

5 This is the *biggest/bigger* room in the hotel.

6 The airport transfer is the *least/most* difficult option. We go straight to the airport from the hotel.

7 It was the *least/worst* meal we ate on holiday!

8 The *furthest/further* we walked was 20 kilometres!

9 Our room has *the best/best* sea view in the hotel.

10 This is *a/the* noisiest restaurant in town.

4 **Complete the text with the superlative form of the adjectives in brackets.**

> Near to Odetta, which is [1]_____ (old) town in the area, you can find [2]_____ (high) mountains in the country. At the bottom of these mountains, we also have [3]_____ (big) forest in the country. Visitors can get lost in there if they don't take a good map!
>
> There are lots of hotels in this area. [4]_____ (expensive) hotel is near the nature park. It doesn't cost a lot because the rooms are quite small. [5]_____ (expensive) hotel, called 'The Prandor', is next to the lake in the middle of the forest. It costs a lot because every room has a wonderful view. People say that the hotel has [6]_____ (beautiful) view in the country because you can see the forest, the lake and the mountains all at the same time. This hotel is also [7]_____ (popular) one in the area. Many people choose to stay there.
>
> There are a lot of walks in the mountains, but it is important to be safe. [8]_____ (safe) option is to walk with a local guide. Many people say that the top of the mountains is [9]_____ (peaceful) place in the area. You can only hear the birds and the wind in the trees!

5 **Correct the mistake in each sentence.**

 the
1 This is easiest way to get to the hotel.

2 I'm having the most worst holiday! It's so boring here.

3 The more interesting place I've been to is Antarctica.

4 Why did you book the least small room in the hotel?

5 The most better restaurants are in this road.

6 It's the quieter hotel in the city, but it's also the most boring.

7 Hostels aren't always a cheapest option.

8 This hotel is the more beautiful one on the island.

3c

Vocabulary

Verb phrases

1 **Choose the correct alternatives.**

1 Children *learn/know* to swim at school.

2 I never *fall/do* asleep on the bus.
I always read a book.

3 She can't *eat/drink* sushi with chopsticks.

4 Can you *do/cook* our meal tonight?
I'm tired!

5 They want to *go/play* skiing in the winter.

6 We can *watch/share* our holiday photos online.

7 He *rides/goes* his bike to work every day.

8 Let's *visit/go* the British Museum when we go to London.

2 **Complete the sentences with the verbs in the box.**

be   break   cook   drive   fall   go
learn   watch

1 I couldn't .... asleep last night because I wasn't tired.

2 I would like to .... a sports car one day.

3 Let's .... the film on my tablet.

4 I don't want to .... a meal this evening. Let's go out.

5 My brother asked me to .... skiing with him next winter.

6 Try not to .... your leg when you go skiing!

7 The students want to .... to speak English very well.

8 Some people want to .... on TV, but I don't.

Grammar

Present perfect with *ever* and *never*

3a **Complete the missing verbs.**

1 Has your sister ever w............... a football match?

2 Have you ever e............... with chopsticks?

3 Have your friends ever s............... a bad photo of you online?

4 Have you ever f............... asleep at the cinema?

5 Has your husband ever l............... to speak another language?

b **Complete the answers with *have, haven't, has* or *hasn't*.**

a Yes, they .... I was really embarrassed.

b No, I .... I prefer using a knife and fork!

c No, she .... She hates sport.

d Yes, he .... He learnt to speak a bit of Russian for a business trip.

e No I .... I love watching films.

c **Match the answers in Exercise 3b with the questions in Exercise 3a.**

1 ....   2 ....   3 ....   4 ....   5 ....

4 **Choose the correct alternatives.**

1 A: Have you *ever/never* broken a bone?

2 B: Yes, I *do/have*. I broke my arm skiing last year.

3 A: I haven't *ever/never* driven a sports car.
B: Really? I *have/haven't*. My sister has one. It's so much fun!

4 A: I've *ever/never* learnt how to ride a bike. Now, I think I'm too old to try.
B: No, you're not! I only *learn/learnt* how to swim last year.

5 A: Karen *gave/given* a great party last weekend. You missed it!
B: Really? I didn't know about it. I've never *went/been* to her house.

5 **Complete the messages with the present perfect or past simple form of the verbs in brackets.**

Tina

Hi there! My husband and I have just moved to the area and we are really excited to join this group! We ¹ .... (never live) in this part of London before. We would like to know about good restaurants in the area. ² .... anyone .... (ever eat) at the Italian restaurant *Mamma Mia's*?

Max

Hi Tina, welcome to the neighbourhood! I ³ .... (go to) *Mamma Mia's* once. I ⁴ .... (not have) a good experience. I had to wait a long time for my food. ⁵ .... you .... (ever try) Indian food? The food at *The Blue Sapphire* is great!

Holly

Hello, Holly here. I ⁶ .... (eat) at *Mamma Mia's* many times and I think it's wonderful. I don't know what happened when Max went there. My experience is that they are always friendly and helpful. Another good Italian restaurant is *Neapolitan*.

Richie

Hey Tina. I ⁷ .... (never go to) *Mamma Mia's*, but I ⁸ .... (try) *The Blue Sapphire* last week. The food is amazing! It's more expensive than some other restaurants, but I think it's the best restaurant in the area.

Functional language

Give and respond to news

1 Complete the conversation with responses a–f.

A: Allen! Hi!

B: **1** *d*

A: Good, thanks. I've just sold my house.

B: **2** ....

A: I wanted to move somewhere quieter, with more green spaces.

B: **3** ....

A: Why? I thought you liked living here.

B: I did! But we have new neighbours and they party all night, every night!

A: **4** ....

B: Yes, I have. But they won't stop.

A: Oh no, sorry to hear that.

B: **5** .... We have some good news.

A: What?

B: Rebecca and I are having a baby!

A: **6** ....

B: Thanks! We don't know yet!

a Lucky you! I'd love to move, too!

b Really? Congratulations! Boy or girl?

c That's fantastic news! Why did you sell?

d Hi, Stuart! How are things?

e That's awful! Have you spoken to them about it?

f Guess what!

2 Match sentences 1–8 with responses a–h.

1 I've lost my phone. I can't find it anywhere! ....

2 Did you hear about Pam and Kevin? They've sold their house. ....

3 Guess what! George asked me to marry him! ....

4 Have you heard about Hugo? He lost his job. ....

5 I got a cold last week and I had to stay in bed for two days. ....

6 Sorry, but I have to cancel our plans for tonight. I have to work late. ....

7 Did you hear that a new sushi restaurant has opened in our area? ....

8 We've booked our holiday! We're going to Malta for two weeks! ....

a Oh, that's fantastic news! When's the big day?

b Sounds amazing! You'll have a fantastic time!

c That's a shame. Are you free tomorrow night?

d Oh, no, sorry to hear that! Maybe you left it at home?

e That's great! We need more restaurants around here.

f That's awful! He was so happy working there.

g Really? That's a surprise! I thought they loved living in Cambridge.

h Oh, what a shame! How are you feeling now?

Listening

1 ◀)) 3.01 **Listen to Jen and Angus discussing a holiday. Write Jen (J), Angus (A) or both (J/A).**

1 .... has been on holiday.

2 .... likes skiing.

3 .... has friends who like hot weather.

4 .... likes being alone.

5 .... likes talking to people.

6 .... took lots of photos.

2 Listen again. Are the sentences true (T) or false (F)?

1 Angus is unhappy his holiday has ended. ....

2 He has been on a skiing holiday to Ben Nevis. ....

3 He spent a week there. ....

4 He liked the holiday because he could practise his skiing and be alone. ....

5 The ski centre is not cheap. ....

6 There are lots of places to eat. ....

7 There are wonderful views. ....

8 It is about four hours' drive from Edinburgh. ....

3a Choose the correct option, a or b.

1 Angus went to Fort William ...
   a by plane.   b by train.

2 Jen ...
   a has been skiing before.
   b has never been skiing before.

3 Jen is surprised that ...
   a Angus went skiing.   b Angus went alone.

4 Angus ...
   a doesn't go skiing often.   b goes skiing regularly.

5 At the end of the conversation ...
   a Jen wants to go skiing for her next holiday.
   b Jen doesn't want to go skiing for her next holiday.

b Listen again and check.

Reading

1 Read the blog post. What's it about?

   a where to go for summer holidays

   b where to go for winter holidays

   c cheap holidays

2 Are the sentences true (T) or false (F)?

   1 The article says that winter holidays are not popular. ....

   2 London in September is 5–10°C. ....

   3 Gozo is a good place for swimming. ....

   4 The world-famous Medina is a beach. ....

   5 It isn't difficult to find cheap places to stay in Marrakech. ....

   6 It takes a long time to travel to the countryside from Las Palmas. ....

   7 Paphos is only good to visit in winter. ....

   8 You can do sea sports in Paphos. ....

3 Read the blog post again. Complete the sentences about the writer's opinions. Write Gozo (G), Marrakech (M), Las Palmas (LP) or Paphos (P).

   1 .... has the best shopping opportunities.

   2 .... is colder than Paphos.

   3 .... has useful public transport.

   4 .... is the best place to really relax.

   5 .... is a great place to visit at other times of the year, too.

   6 .... is good value for money.

   7 .... is the hottest.

   8 .... has a famous place.

4 Look at the underlined words. Choose the option which has a similar meaning.

   1 You can jump on a plane (paragraph 1)

     a get on a plane quickly

     b get on a plane slowly

   2 You can enjoy a comfortable 20°C (paragraph 2)

     a the weather is too hot

     b the weather is relaxing

   3 It's smaller than Malta and also greener. (paragraph 2)

     a it has more nature

     b it has less nature

   4 jewellery made by local people (paragraph 3)

     a people who live close to the area

     b people who come from different parts of the country

   5 It has become the go-to place for fans of warm-weather sports. (paragraph 5)

     a popular

     b unpopular

We work hard all year long, so when it's time for a holiday it's a big decision. We need to think about where to go, when to go and how much to spend. Most people go on holiday in the summer months, but these days many people are starting to take their holidays in the winter months. Why be cold and unhappy in the UK when you can jump on a plane and be in the sun in just a few hours? This is what many of us think. But where are the best places to visit at this time of year?

Gozo, Malta (3 hours)

London in November is a cold 5–10°C. But just three hours by plane and you can enjoy a comfortable 20°C on the beautiful Island of Gozo, in Malta. This quiet and peaceful place has beautiful beaches and amazing views. Do you like swimming in the sea? Gozo has some of the best swimming in the Mediterranean and the water is not too cold. It's smaller than Malta and also greener. It's the perfect winter holiday.

Marrakech, Morocco (4 hours)

Marrakech is a city with a lot of history. The temperature is 23°C in November, which is the perfect weather to enjoy the world-famous Medina market. This is a 19-kilometre street market where you can buy any kind of food, furniture, art and jewellery made by local people. It's easy to find cheap accommodation in Marrakech. The local hotels are called *riads* and are much cheaper than normal hotels. They're usually very quiet and comfortable, too!

Las Palmas, Gran Canaria (4 hours)

The city of Las Palmas has some beautiful streets and lots of interesting buildings, museums, cafés and theatres. It also has beautiful countryside outside of the city. Take a short bus ride and you can go for a good walk, and enjoy the sun and fresh air. You can also relax on one of its five amazing beaches and enjoy the 24°C temperature. Not bad for 'winter'!

Paphos, Cyprus (4.5 hours)

A trip to Paphos is good at any time of year, but it's a great winter destination, especially if you enjoy having fun. Have you ever been surfing? Do you like riding a bike or mountain climbing? You can do all of these things in November in Paphos. Because of its beautiful National Park, restaurants and warm weather (22°C), Paphos has become the go-to place for people who like warm-weather sports.

Writing

1 **Read the review of a day trip. What's the reviewer's opinion of the trip?**

  a The trip was too short.

  b The trip was boring.

  c The trip was interesting.

⊙⊙⊙⊙◯ Reviewed yesterday

I booked an organised day trip to Bath with AS Tours in June. I went with my cousin from America. The city has a lot of history and is famous for its Roman Baths.

The whole day trip takes 12 hours. We went by train and left Victoria station at 8 a.m. It only takes an hour and a half to get to Bath. A guide takes you to different places and gives you lots of interesting information.

The trip begins with a visit to the Botanical Gardens, where you can see lots of trees and flowers. We spent two hours in the gardens. Then we walked to the Jane Austen Centre to learn about the famous writer. We had one hour there and after that we had lunch. Lunch is included in the trip and is served in a hotel in the centre of Bath. After lunch, there was a tour of Bath Abbey, followed by a tour of the Roman Baths. It was a really interesting day and my cousin loved it!

The only problem was the timing. We had too much time in the gardens and not enough time for visiting the other places. The visit to the Abbey was too short and we didn't have enough time to enjoy the famous Roman Baths. I wanted to take more photos, but we had to go because our train back to London was at 6.30 p.m.

It's a long day and there's lots of walking, so it's important to wear a comfortable pair of shoes, but Bath is a beautiful city and it's full of history. So, if you enjoy learning about history, this trip is for you!

2 **Read the review again. Are the sentences true (T) or false (F)?**

  1 AS Tours plan the whole day for you. _____

  2 The journey takes one and a half hours by coach. _____

  3 You spend the same amount of time in the Botanical Gardens and in the Jane Austen Centre. _____

  4 The group can choose where to have lunch. _____

  5 The reviewer thinks that they spent too much time in the gardens. _____

  6 You will like this trip if you enjoy walking and history. _____

3 **Read the Focus box. Then put sentences a–d below in the correct order.**

Organising ideas

It's important to organise your ideas well so your readers can follow them clearly. For example, in a review of a day trip, you could organise your ideas like this:

1 Where, when, who with
I booked an organised day trip to Bath with AS Tours in June.

2 General information/positive things
The trip begins with a visit to the Botanical Gardens.

3 Any problems
The only problem was the timing.

4 Recommendations
So, if you enjoy learning about history, this trip is for you!

  a We weren't happy to pay extra to go into the castle. _____

  b I booked an organised day trip to Windsor with Happy Tours in May. _____

  c Windsor is a small and pretty town with a lot of shops and a castle. If you enjoy shopping, sightseeing and culture, you'll love this town! _____

  d The day trip includes a guided walking tour around the small streets and the castle. _____

Prepare

4 **Think about a day trip you have taken. Make notes about the questions below.**

  • Where did you go, when did you go there, who did you go with?

  • What did you do during the day trip?

  • What went well and what went badly?

  • What recommendations do you have for someone else taking the same day trip?

Write

5 **Write your review of the day trip. Organise your ideas clearly. Use your notes in Exercise 4 and the Focus box to help you.**

4A

Vocabulary

Celebrations

1 **Choose the correct alternatives.**

I really love a good public **1**_party/ holiday_. My country, Chile, has 14 of them! My favourite is Independence Day. It's a traditional **2**_festival/ celebrate_ for the whole country. On this day, we eat our national food. Some people cook at home and **3**_make/ have_ dinner parties. Other people prefer to **4**_have/ do_ fun in the street. Everyone eats lots of empanadas!

Every year I **5**_celebrate/ party_ my birthday. It's my favourite celebration. I like it because I can **6**_get/ go_ together with old friends and family and spend time with them. Sometimes, I **7**_talk/ contact_ old friends from school and we **8**_go out/ have_ for a meal in a good restaurant and **9**_get/ have_ a dinner party. People **10**_give/ have_ gifts and it makes me feel really special.

2 **Match questions 1–6 with responses a–f.**

1 Do you prefer giving or receiving gifts?

    ....

2 What do you do to have fun? ....

3 How often do you get together with friends? ....

4 How are you going to celebrate your birthday? ....

5 Shall we go out for a meal tonight? ....

6 Why are you spending so much time online? ....

a I like going dancing with friends.

b That's a good idea!

c Once or twice a week.

d I'm trying to contact an old friend.

e Getting presents of course!

f I'm having a dinner party.

Grammar

be going to, want and *would like*

3 **Complete the conversation with the words in the box.**

> 'd like to   doesn't want   going to   like to   'm going to   're going to be   to do   want   wants

A: So, what are you **1**_____ do for your mum's birthday this year?

B: Well, we **2**_____ to go to her favourite restaurant for lunch. It's her 60th, so I **3**_____ to make it really special.

A: Oh, that sounds nice. Are you going **4**_____ anything in the evening as well?

B: Yes. I know she **5**_____ see all her friends, but she **6**_____ to go out, so I **7**_____ organise a small party at home. And my brother **8**_____ to make her a big birthday cake! Would you **9**_____ come to the party?

A: I would, but I'm going **10**_____ on holiday in France! I hope you have a lovely time.

4 **Put the words in the correct order to make sentences.**

1 next / finish / month / going / I'm / to / university
   I'm going to finish university next month.

2 I'd / to / like / hour / leave / in / an

3 I'm / going / see / to / tomorrow / the / day / her / after

4 like / to / Would / you / have / with / me / Saturday / dinner / this?

5 I / go / don't / to / tonight / want / out

6 meet / Can / me / tomorrow / four o'clock / you / at?

7 an / do / course / going / year / to / English / next / I'm

5 **Correct the mistake in each sentence.**

   wants

1 Jack ~~want~~ to have a dinner party next week.

2 I'd like go out for a meal this Friday.

3 Tonight, I like to stay home and watch a film.

4 I'm tired, so I not going to go out tonight.

5 Can you call John? He want to speak to you.

6 It's your mum's birthday next week. How do you going to celebrate?

7 I no want to get a job after university. I want to travel!

8 This party is boring and I want go home.

Grammar

will/*won't* for decisions and offers

1 Match sentences 1–6 with responses a–f.

1 Who made all this mess in the kitchen? ....
2 When are you coming home? I'm bored. ....
3 There's a problem with the trains today. ....
4 Mum, I can't find my shoes! ....
5 I need to buy some milk after work today. ....
6 It's raining outside. ....

a Oh no! I'll take the bus to work instead.
b Thanks for letting me know. I'll take an umbrella.
c I won't be long, I'll leave soon.
d I'll help you find them.
e Sorry, that was me. I'll clean it up now.
f OK, I'll send you a text later to remind you.

2 Correct the mistake in each sentence.

won't

1 I~~no~~ go for a run today, it's really cold outside!

2 Do you need some help with your homework? I help you!

3 It's very noisy outside – I'll closing the window.

4 I'm hungry, I think I'll to cook dinner early tonight.

5 It's Jenny's birthday next week. I'll bought her a present.

6 I've got a lot of work to do tomorrow – I won't staying out late tonight.

3 Use the prompts to write responses with *will* or *won't*.

1 **A:** What time will you be home? It's late!
   B: I / know! / I / leave / the office / soon
      I know! I'll leave the office soon.

2 **A:** That's the phone.
   B: I / answer / it

3 **A:** These bags are very heavy.
   B: I / carry / them

4 **A:** You took my car without asking me.
   B: I / not / do / it / again

5 **A:** I bought flowers for Tanya's birthday.
   B: I / not / buy / any / then

6 **A:** We need lots of food for the party on Friday!
   B: Don't worry / I / bring / some

Vocabulary

Organising events

4 Choose the correct alternatives.

> **How to organise a party**
>
> First, you need to ¹*make/set/remind* a date and ²*bake/send/choose* a place to have your party. It's a good idea to ³*make/set/book* some food or people might get hungry. You could make sandwiches or even ⁴*plan/choose/bake* a cake! If you want to have music, you could ⁵*remind/book/choose* a DJ or a band. Another fun idea is to ⁶*bake/set/plan* some activities for people to do. Then you should tell people about the party. Some people just email guests or call them, but I think it's much nicer if you ⁷*send/remind/choose* invitations. Finally, it's a good idea if you ⁸*make/book/remind* people about the party one week before. You don't want people to forget about it!

5 Match the sentence halves.

1 We need to book a band, ...
2 We can buy a cake or ....
3 We should set a date soon then ....
4 It's an important celebration wth lots of people, ...
5 I want to send invitations ....
6 We can make food, ...
7 We should remind people one week before, ...
8 We want people to have fun, ...

a people can keep the evening free.
b by email because it's cheaper.
c so we should choose a big place.
d so people can dance.
e so they don't forget.
f so we should plan some games.
g we can bake one.
h so people won't get hungry.

4c

Grammar

can, can't, have to, don't have to

1 **Choose the correct alternatives.**

A: Hello, FitU gym. How can I help?

B: Hi. I'd like some information about your classes. How much **1**_do I have to/can I_ pay?

A: Are you a member?

B: Yes, I joined last week.

A: OK, members **2**_can't/don't have to_ pay extra for classes.

B: Oh, good! **3**_Do I have to/Can I_ be very fit?

A: No. Beginners **4**_can/can't_ take different classes.

B: When are the classes?

A: Morning classes are on Tuesdays and Thursdays at 7 a.m.

B: I **5**_can/can't_ come then. It's too early for me.

A: No problem. We also have evening classes on Mondays and Wednesdays at 6 p.m.

B: Good. **6**_Can I/Do I have_ to book first?

A: Yes, you **7**_have to/can't_ book. You **8**_can/don't have to_ use our website.

B: Thank you.

2 **Write the second sentence so it has the same meaning as the first sentence. Use _can, can't, have to_ or _don't have to_.**

1 It is necessary to sign a 12-month contract.
You _____ sign a 12-month contract.

2 It is possible to cancel your membership in the first month.
You _____ cancel your membership in the first month.

3 It is not necessary to bring your own towel because the gym provides you with one.
You _____ bring your own towel because the gym provides you with one.

4 It is not possible to bring food into the gym from outside.
You _____ bring food into the gym from outside.

5 If you lose your membership card, it is necessary to pay £5 for a new one.
If you lose your membership card, you _____ pay £5 for a new one.

6 With your membership card, it is possible to use any London club.
With your membership card, you _____ use any London club.

3 **Complete the texts with _can, can't, have to_ or _don't have to_ and the verbs in brackets.**

NEW GYM CLASSES!

Bikebodyplus	SpiritYoga
Feel the music and go, go, go! Our cycle class is perfect for everyone. You **1**_____ (have) previous experience. With bikebodyplus classes, you **2**_____ (get) fit very quickly. You **3**_____ (bring) any special equipment. Just come! Ride with us today! Wednesday, 7–8 p.m.	This is a class for advanced yoga students only. You **4**_____ (be) very strong and flexible. Our instructors **5**_____ (help) you improve your yoga and reduce your stress. You **6**_____ (bring) a yoga mat because we provide them at every class. Wednesday, 6–7 p.m.

Vocabulary

-ed and -ing adjectives

4 **Match the definitions with the words in the box.**

bored   excited   interested   relaxed   surprised   tired   worried

1 You feel very enthusiastic and happy. _____
2 You feel unhappy because something is not interesting. _____
3 You like something and want to know more about it. _____
4 You feel this when you think about your problems. _____
5 You feel this when something happens that you did not expect.
 _____
6 You feel happy because nothing is worrying you. _____
7 You feel like you want to rest or sleep. _____

5 **Complete the sentences with the adjectives in the box.**

~~boring/bored~~   exciting/excited   interested/interesting   relaxing/relaxed   surprising/surprised   tiring/tired   worrying/worried

1 a I don't enjoy running and I think it's really _boring_ .
  b I feel _bored_ when I go running.
2 a I like watching football, but playing it is more _____ .
  b I get _____ when I play football.
3 a I love yoga. It makes me feel really _____ .
  b I love yoga. It's really _____ .
4 a I tried a class at my local gym and it was really _____ .
  b I tried a class at my local gym and I was really _____ .
5 a I didn't think I would like Pilates. I was really _____ that I loved it!
  b I didn't think I would like Pilates. It was really _____ that I loved it!
6 a I'm really _____ about the bad news Helen told me.
  b The bad news Helen told me was really _____ .
7 a I think sport science is really _____ .
  b I'm really _____ in sport science.

Functional language

Make invitations and plans to meet

1 Complete the conversations with the words in the boxes.

> good   let's   like   love   shall

A: We're going to the theatre on Saturday. Would you **1**_____ to come?

B: I'd **2**_____ to! Where **3**_____ we meet?

A: **4**_____ meet in front of the theatre. The play starts at eight o'clock, so how about 7.45?

B: Great! That's a **5**_____ idea. I'll buy a ticket. See you then!

> busy   join   think   want

A: I'm going shopping in town. Do you want to **6**_____ me?

B: No, I don't **7**_____ I can, sorry. I've got too much work to do.

A: Oh, that's a shame. Do you **8**_____ to meet up later for a coffee?

B: I'm sorry I can't, I'm **9**_____ then, too. Maybe tomorrow?

> can   meet   sounds   sure

A: Shall we **10**_____ at seven o'clock in front of the stadium?

B: I'm not **11**_____ about that. It'll be so busy.

A: What about six o'clock then?

B: Sorry, I don't think I **12**_____ because I only finish work at six. Let's meet inside the stadium.

A: Yes, that **13**_____ fine. I'll see you in there.

2 Choose the correct alternatives.

1 We're going to the Italian restaurant tomorrow. Do you want *join/ to join* us?

2 I'd *love to/ love* go with you to the new shopping centre.

3 I'm not *sure/ think* about taking the train. The bus is cheaper.

4 Do you want *meeting/ to meet* for a coffee soon?

5 Where shall we *meeting/ meet* up this evening?

6 Thanks for the invitation, but I *don't/ not* think I can.

7 Taking the car is a *good/ best* idea. It's much faster.

8 *Let's/ Let* meet in front of the school after class.

9 I'm going swimming. Do you *come/ want* to join me?

10 It's good of you to ask, but *I/ I'm* busy for the whole weekend.

11 That *sound/ sounds* like a great idea – I'll see you tomorrow.

12 So that we have time to chat, *shall/ let's* we meet an hour before it starts?

Listening

1 🔊 4.01 **Listen to a discussion about a celebration. Why are they planning the celebration?**

a It's someone's birthday.

b It's the company's birthday.

c Someone in the company is leaving.

2 **Listen again. Are the sentences true (T) or false (F)?**

1 The event is next week. _____

2 They're planning an evening-only celebration. _____

3 The company is 50 years old. _____

4 They would like a small venue for the celebration. _____

5 Everyone thinks that cricket is a good activity. _____

6 Jess says that not everyone likes sport. _____

7 Danny has never been to a murder mystery day. _____

8 There aren't actors on the murder mystery day. _____

3a **Choose the correct alternatives.**

1 They want to have *dinner/ activities* for everyone.

2 Danny thinks it's going to be *difficult/ easy* to find something for everyone.

3 Pauline thinks sport is a *bad/ good* idea.

4 The people at a murder mystery party are the *detectives/ actors*.

5 The detectives *choose/ guess* who the murderer is.

6 Pauline is going to *find the venue/ plan the food*.

7 Danny is going to *book/ talk to* the actors.

8 Next week they are going to *plan/ prepare* the evening celebration.

b **Listen again and check.**

Reading

1 Read the article. What does an events organiser do?
a decides if you will have a party
b gives you a score after your party
c helps you plan your party

The perfect celebration?

I'm spending the morning with Elena, an events organiser, at a top hotel in London. Elena is waiting for her first client. She has a **folder** full of event venues, price lists and ideas. I'm going to find out what she's going to plan and what she really thinks!

The client arrives 15 minutes late. It is clear that she is very rich. She is wearing expensive clothes and two diamond rings. She wants to plan a big celebration for her husband's birthday.

'I want the biggest and the best of everything!' she says. 'It has to be the party of the year. It can't be anything else! The party is in two weeks' time.' Elena and her client speak for two hours. Elena keeps smiling. Finally, the client leaves. Now I want to know what Elena really thinks.

'This client asked me to bake the best cake, find a big **venue**, book a famous DJ, send the most beautiful invitations, and she wants me to do this in two weeks!' laughs Elena.

'Can you do everything your client wants?' I ask.

'It's **impossible**! But I think I can book a good venue and prepare wonderful food. Then I'll tell her that everything is the best!' says Elena, and she gives me a big smile.

'Is it going to be OK, do you think?' I ask.

'Of course it will be OK. The party will be a lot of fun.' Elena picks up her folder, makes a phone call and then leaves.

A couple of days before the party, I visit Elena's client. I want to find out what she thinks. I ask her about Elena's planning.

'It's great!' she says. 'It's going to be the best celebration with excellent food, in an amazing place.'

I ask the client if she thinks Elena has organised everything well.

'Very well,' she says. 'It is important to me that the celebration is **perfect**. I know that Elena can organise this!'

I can see that Elena is very good at her job. She's doing everything she can to make this celebration **a night to remember**!

2 Read the article again. Choose the correct alternatives.
1 The writer meets Elena in the *morning/ evening*.
2 The writer *leaves before/ stays when* the clients arrives.
3 The client wants Elena to arrange *a better party than the one last year/ the best party this year*.
4 Elena *is/ isn't* able to do everything the client asks for.
5 The client thinks Elena *can/ can't* do everything she's asked for.

3 Read the article again. Correct one word in each sentence.
has
1 The event organiser ~~hasn't~~ got a folder with lots of useful information.

2 Elena says that it's possible to give the client what she says she wants.

3 The client arrives early for the meeting.

4 Two weeks is enough time to do everything the client asks for.

5 Elena is worried about the celebration.

6 The client thinks that Elena isn't a good events organiser.

7 The writer thinks that the celebration isn't going to be a success.

4 Match the words in bold in the article with meanings 1–5.
1 an evening you will never forget
   ....
2 something that cannot be done
   ....
3 a cover made of paper or plastic to carry papers
   ....
4 something that is the best or as good as it can be
   ....
5 a place where an organised event happens
   ....

4

Writing

1 Reads the invitations and match headings a–c with gaps 1–3.

   a My birthday party

   b Surprise party

   c Wedding celebration

---

1 ....

After 40 years of working as a doctor, Mum's going to stop work and retire next month. We're organising a celebration party for her. She doesn't know about it, so please keep it secret.

The party will be in *Jose's Joint*, on 4th July at 7 p.m.

This is her favourite restaurant and it's got great food and live music.

We'd love you to come, and we know Mum would, too!

Please let me know so I can book the table.

Remember, it's a secret!

---

2 ....

Hi Lisa, it's my birthday next week and I'm going to have a small party to celebrate. The party will be at my flat, which is 100 Butterfly Gardens, West Road. There will be food, drink and good music! I'd love you to come if you're free. It will start at 8 p.m. and continue until late. And you don't have to get me a present! Please let me know if you can come so I know how much food and drink to buy. I really hope you can make it!

---

3 ....

Pete and Gemma's big day is only a few months away now and I'm organising Gemma's hen party, her party before the wedding, for 11th June. We're going to go to a spa hotel during the day. We can have a relaxing time there. Then we're going to have a salsa class at a dance studio and then go out for dinner. Finally, we'll go to Gemma's favourite club.

I hope you can make it.

2 Read the invitations again. Which invitation (1, 2 or 3) ...

   a is for someone who is finishing work forever? ....

   b is in someone's home? ....

   c has a dance class? ....

   d has live music in the restaurant? ....

   e has a relaxing part in the day? ....

   f is from 8 p.m. until late? ....

3 Read the Focus box. Which phrases in the box are in the invitations in Exercise 1?

Inviting and responding

You can use some specific phrases when you write an invitation in English.

We'd love you to come.   I hope you can make it.

You can also use similar phrases when responding to an invitation.

We'd love to come.   Of course we'll be there!

If you can't accept an invitation, it's always a good idea to say why and use expressions like *but unfortunately*, *I'm afraid* and *have fun/a great time*, to be more polite.

Sorry, but unfortunately, we can't make it. We're on holiday then.

I'm afraid I can't come – it's my sister's birthday. Have a great time!

4 Choose the correct alternatives.

   1 The party is next Saturday and we'd *hope/love* you to come.

   2 Your plans sound great, but *afraid/unfortunately* I've got to work on that day.

   3 Everything is booked for 10th April and we'd love you *to come/come* and join us.

   4 It sounds great, but I'm *unfortunately/afraid* I'm on holiday then.

   5 Unfortunately we can't be there for your 40th birthday, but *have/make* a great time.

   6 Thanks for the invite. Of course we'll *be there/go there*!

5 Complete the reply to an invitation with one word in each gap.

Thanks so much for inviting me to your party.
I **1**.................. love to come, but **2**.................. I can't make it on 3rd August. I'm **3**.................. I'm on holiday in France then. Have a great **4**.................. . I'm so sorry that I can't **5**.................. it.

Prepare

6 You're going to reply to the invitations in Exercise 1. Decide which one you will accept, and which two you will not accept. Think about what you will say in your replies and make notes.

Write

7 Write your replies to the invitations in Exercise 1. Give reasons for not accepting two of the invitations. Use the phrases in the Focus box to help you.

Vocabulary

Job skills and preferences

1 **Complete the sentences with the words and phrases in the box.**

communication   creative   customers   from home
long hours   part-time   team   well-paid

1 As an engineer you have to be _____
   and also good with numbers.

2 It is important to be friendly when you work in a shop
   with _____ .

3 Sue wants to earn a lot of money, so she is looking for
   a job that is _____ .

4 Tracy doesn't need to travel to work because she works
   _____ .

5 I work _____ so that I also have some
   time for my family.

6 A doctor works with a lot of people and needs to have
   good _____ skills.

7 I don't have much free time because I work
   _____ .

8 I enjoy working in a _____ because
   I think it's good to share ideas.

2 **Choose the correct alternatives.**

1 **A:** Are you still working *part-time/on your own* at the
   shopping centre?
   B: No, I left last month. My boss wasn't a *good manager/
   communication skills*, so I didn't enjoy it. Now I'm
   working from *a team/home* and I love it!

2 **A:** I can finally buy my own home! I've got a new job that
   is *well-paid/part-time*.
   B: Oh, that's great! Do you have to work *long hours/
   creative*?
   A: No, I don't. I work in a *customers/team*, and we help
   each other.

3 **A:** I want to change my job because I have to work
   a good manager/on my own and I don't enjoy it!
   B: You're great with people. You should work
   with customers/long hours.
   A: That's a good idea because I think I have good
   creative/communication skills.

Grammar

Relative clauses with *who, which* and *that*

3 **Choose the correct alternatives.**

1 A zoo keeper is a person *who/which* looks after animals.
2 He's the guitarist *who/which* plays in our band.
3 We need a car *who/which* can go fast.
4 Is that the coat *who/which* your husband bought you
   for your birthday?
5 The train on platform three is the one *who/which* goes
   to the airport.
6 She's the hairdresser *who/which* did my hair for my
   sister's wedding.
7 This is the book *who/which* I started reading last week.
8 These are the tools *who/which* you need to put up
   the shelf.
9 It's a job *who/which* pays a lot of money.
10 Sara's aunt is the woman *who/which* won the singing
   competition.

4 **Put the words and phrases in the correct order to make
sentences.**

1 helped you / Is that / who / the boy?
   _____

2 a ship / A cruise / is on / which / is a holiday
   _____

3 which / is / something / A straw / for drinking / you can use
   _____

4 is the player / the trophy / won / Roger / who
   _____

5 the dress / That's / to the party / I wore / which
   _____

6 who / is now / Stella / is the person / the manager
   _____

5 **Match the sentences halves.**

1 An accountant is a person _____
2 A map is something _____
3 A reporter is a person _____
4 This is the charity _____
5 A dictionary is a book _____
6 This is the friend _____
7 Is that the dentist _____
8 Paella is the dish _____

a who writes news stories.
b who looked at your teeth last week?
c which gives the meanings of words.
d who can help you look after your money.
e who went on holiday with me.
f which can help you when you are lost.
g which helps people who don't have money.
h which I cook on special days.

Grammar

look like/look + adjective/be like

1 Choose the correct alternatives.

1 Ana *looks/looks like* that famous actress.
2 What's wrong? You *look/are like* really angry.
3 She can't be the new boss. She *looks/looks like* really young!
4 What does the new football shirt *look like/be like?*
5 What does Tim's new girlfriend *look/look like?*
6 That food *looks/looks like* very tasty.
7 Tess always *looks/is like* bored in class.
8 Stephen *looks/looks like* really tired after his long run.
9 Do you *look like/look* your mother or your father?
10 What are your new colleagues *like/look like?*

2 Put the words and phrases in the correct order to make sentences.

1 looks like / an athlete / Shelly / is very fit and
_____
2 happy / keeps smiling and / Greg / looks / really
_____
3 like / What / look / your sister / does?
_____
4 really nervous / Everyone / looked / on the first day
_____
5 and Jo / look like / sisters / Cindy
_____
6 his father / Peter / looks like / and his grandfather
_____
7 and unhappy / looks / Karen / today / very tired
_____
8 new girlfriend / like / What's / Ben's?
_____

3 Complete the sentences with the correct form of *look like, look* or *be like.*

1 Your car _____ new! Is it really second-hand?
2 What does the new hotel in town _____?
3 She's very beautiful and _____ a model.
4 I think that something is wrong because they _____ really sad!
5 Bob _____ he's in his mid-forties.
6 What _____ your new flatmate _____? Is he friendly?
7 Your dog _____ hot. Shall I get some water for him?
8 What does your new flat _____?
9 Do you know what the film _____?
10 What _____ your new boss _____? Is he nicer than the last one?

Vocabulary

Appearance

4 Complete the sentences with the words in the box.

bald   blonde   dark   long   moustache   slim
smart   tall   tattoo

1 Many people in Scandinavia have _____ hair and blue eyes.
2 Last year he had _____ hair, but now it's quite short.
3 I've lost a lot of weight, so now I'm quite _____.
4 My dad is _____ now – he doesn't have any hair!
5 That actress has beautiful _____ brown hair and eyes.
6 Basketball players are usually _____.
7 Eva has an interview, so she's wearing a _____ dress and jacket.
8 She's got a _____ of a dragon on her arm.
9 Do you think I'd look good with a _____ and beard?

5 Choose the correct alternatives.

1 He's got short brown hair and it's very *straight/long.*
2 He's very *casual/smart* – he always wears a shirt and tie.
3 I need a *long/tall* person to help me reach the top shelf.
4 I'm thinking of cutting my hair *curly/short.*
5 This kind of dog is usually *slim/straight* so that it can run fast.
6 He's *bald/smart* – he lost his hair in his 20s.
7 Jose's *dark/blonde* hair and eyes makes him look different from his brother.
8 I prefer *casual/smart* clothes. I'm happy in jeans and a T-shirt.
9 When my mother was young, many people had *curly/slim* hair.
10 He's bald, but he has a *beard/curly.*

Vocabulary

Shopping

1 Complete the phrases with the words in the box.

ask   compare   in a   keep   pay   read   return   try

1 .... for a discount
2 .... the receipt
3 .... reviews
4 .... prices
5 .... by credit card
6 .... something
7 .... sale
8 .... something on

2 Match the sentence halves.

1 My sister never reads reviews before ....
2 Most people now pay ....
3 I don't like it when I have to return ....
4 I always buy new trainers when ....
5 It's damaged, so I'm going to ask ....
6 Why didn't you keep ....
7 Before I buy anything I always compare ....
8 My son never likes to try ....

a the receipt for that jacket?
b by credit card rather than with cash.
c clothes on in a shop.
d something I've been given as a present.
e they are cheaper in a sale.
f she buys and sometimes makes a mistake.
g prices to find the cheapest one.
h for a discount.

3 Complete the sentences with the phrases in the box.

ask for a discount   compare prices   in a sale
kept the receipt   pay by credit card
read some reviews   return something   try it on

1 My sister always waits until clothes are cheaper
.... because she wants to save money.
2 I never carry cash. I always ....
3 I'm so happy I .... for the iron I bought last week. It's broken, so I was able to exchange it.
4 .... before you buy it! It might not fit!
5 Let's .... before we buy a new bed so that we don't pay too much.
6 When I go to a market, I always .... to see if they will give me a cheaper price.
7 I always .... before I buy a new phone. I want to know other people's opinions.
8 It is possible to .... to the shop if you don't like it or it doesn't work.

Grammar

should/shouldn't and imperatives

4 Choose the correct option, a or b.

1 She has a cut on her head and .... go to see the nurse.
   a shouldn't   b should
2 .... leave a dog alone in a car on a hot day.
   a Never   b Always
3 Footballers .... have a good rest the night before a big game.
   a shouldn't   b should
4 You .... carry those bags. They're too heavy for you!
   a shouldn't   b should
5 .... eat breakfast because it's the most important meal of the day.
   a Always   b Never
6 You .... go to the theatre to see that show. I think it's wonderful.
   a shouldn't   b should
7 I want to speak better English, so I .... practise every day.
   a shouldn't   b should
8 We .... have a party at our new flat. It's got lots of space.
   a shouldn't   b should
9 We're lost, so we .... look at the map.
   a should   b shouldn't
10 .... brush your teeth after eating. It helps to keep them healthy.
   a Never   b Always

5 Correct the mistake in each sentence.

             wear
1 You should/~~worn~~ a seatbelt in a car.
2 Daphne says I shouldn't worried about my exams.
3 Never leaving a child alone in a swimming pool.
4 You shouldn't telling anyone about the party. It's a secret!
5 I should studying every day.
6 My grandmother says, 'Help always your friends!'
7 You should went to the doctor.
8 Get never in a car with strangers. It's dangerous!
9 Mike should calls his family because they haven't heard from him.
10 Always to wear sun cream when you go to the beach.

Functional language

Make and respond to suggestions

1 **Choose the correct alternatives.**

A: It's my dad's birthday next week, but I don't know what to get him.

B: ¹*How/Why* don't you buy him some socks?

A: No, I got him socks last year! Also, it's an important birthday. He'll be 70!

B: Oh, that is a big birthday. ²*Let's/Should* think about it. I'm sure we can find something!

A: I need to find something he'll really love.

B: You could ³*buy/to buy* him a really nice watch.

A: No, he already has a watch and he likes it.

B: OK, ⁴*where/how* about a nice shirt?

A: Maybe, but I think he'd prefer something more personal.

B: Oh, OK. What does he really enjoy?

A: He loves coffee.

B: I know! Why ⁵*don't/no* you get him one of those new coffee machines?

A: ⁶*That's/It* a fantastic idea!

B: Great! Why don't we ⁷*go/going* to town tomorrow and have a look in the shops?

A: Yes! Let's do that.

2 **Put the words in the correct order to complete the conversations.**

1 **A:** How can I improve my listening skills?
   B: watching / try / You / could / TV

   _____

2 **A:** Can you recommend a good place to visit in London?
   B: the Tower of London / about / How?

   _____

3 **A:** This party is boring.
   B: Let's / home / go

   _____

4 **A:** I don't know what to cook tonight.
   B: steak / What / and / about / chips?

   _____

5 **A:** Do you think the restaurant is open?
   B: don't / Why / ask / you call / and

   _____

6 **A:** Shall we go to the theatre this weekend?
   B: the / cinema / I'd / prefer / I / think / to / go / to

   _____

7 **A:** What shall I get Amy for her birthday?
   B: could / her / nice chocolates / buy / You / some

   _____

8 **A:** Let's go to the cinema on Saturday night.
   B: really / idea / a / OK / good / that's

   _____

Listening

1 🔊 **5.01 Listen to the first part of a job interview and answer the questions.**

1 Which job is the interview for? _____

2 Who will Charlie work for? _____

2 **Listen again. Complete the notes with one word in each gap.**

Name: ¹ *Charlie* Parker

Degree: ² _____ Literature

Current Job: office worker
He enjoys working in a team and he's good with
³ _____ .
He likes his job, but it's ⁴ _____ .
He wants more ⁵ _____ .

Charlie's good qualities:
He's very ⁶ _____ ,
He has good ⁷ _____ skills.
He can ⁸ _____ well.

Typing: He can type ⁹ _____ words a minute.

---

3 🔊 **5.02 Listen to the second part of the interview. Choose the correct alternatives.**

1 Charlie *has/doesn't have* experience working as a PA.

2 Charlie *is happy to/doesn't want to* work long hours.

3 The job *usually/always* starts at 8.30.

4 In the morning, he needs to *check emails/ make phone calls.*

5 Vicky arrives at *9/9.30* a.m.

6 Meetings are *before/after* 12 p.m.

7 Charlie will need to arrange *laptops/food and drink* for the meetings.

8 Charlie *goes/doesn't go* to the meetings.

Reading

1 **Read the article. What is it about?**

a How to save money

b Different ways to shop

c Where to shop

2 **Read the article again. Which of the shoppers ...**

1 wants lots of information about their product? _B_

2 looks for the cheapest products they can, but doesn't ask for discounts? _____

3 asks other people's opinions about a product? _____

4 buys things that they don't need? _____

5 thinks shopping is a fun activity? _____

6 always talks to people in shops? _____

7 doesn't like to change what they buy? _____

8 asks for extra things? _____

9 doesn't worry about money? _____

10 likes to shop with other people? _____

3 **Find words 1–10 in the article. Use the text to help you guess the correct meaning.**

1 waste money (paragraph A)

a spend money in a bad way

b save money for the future

2 special offers (paragraph A)

a when you don't pay full price for something or you get something for free

b when you get the best products for less money

3 models (paragraph B)

a good-looking people

b different types of a product

4 cute (paragraph C)

a very nice, pretty

b cheap, or not too expensive

5 details (paragraph C)

a information   b sizes

6 slightly (paragraph D)

a a lot   b a little

7 give up (paragraph D)

a stop   b start

8 stores (paragraph E)

a products   b shops

9 window shopping (paragraph F)

a buying new windows

b looking but not buying

Shop 'til you drop

Some people love shopping, some people hate it, some do it quickly and some like to relax and enjoy it. There are lots of way of doing it! In this article, we'll tell you about six types of shopper – but which one are you?

A *'I want the best price'*

You don't like to waste money, so when you shop you always want to find the best price you can. You look for special offers in the shops and online, and you don't always need to buy something, you're happy to wait until you find a good price. You go to lots of different shops to compare prices. If you can find what you are looking for in a sale, even better!

B *'I need to know everything'*

You shop very carefully. You need to find out everything about a product before you buy it. You read reviews in magazines and blogs to check what people say, and you talk to friends who own the products, too. You have questions about everything – what sizes are there, how many models do they have, why is this one better than that one? After that, you are ready to go and buy something, and you always keep the receipt!

C *'That's a nice colour'*

You're the opposite of 'I need to know everything'. You're not interested in all the details about a product, and you don't want to spend hours and hours reading about it. When you see something you like, you buy it. Maybe you don't need it, but it's so cute! Maybe you don't have enough money, but that's why you have a credit card, right?

D *'Give me more!'*

You also want to pay less for a product like 'I want the best price', but you are slightly different because you always talk to people in stores and ask them for a discount. If a phone costs £200, you offer £150. If six oranges cost £3, then you ask for a seventh orange for free. You never give up. Sometimes people are a little scared of you!

E *'I know what I like'*

Shopping is easy for you, because you always buy the same thing, the same trainers, the same jeans, the same shoes, even the same food. You know which shops you like, and you only go to those stores. Sometimes people say that you're boring, but you know what makes you happy, so why change?

F *'I shop for fun'*

Shopping isn't only about buying things, it's about spending time with your friends, and looking at all the great things in shop windows. In fact, window shopping is a hobby for you! Sometimes when you go shopping you don't buy anything at all, but you have a great time anyway. Your idea of a good Saturday is spending time with your best friend in the local shopping centre.

Writing

1 Read the guide to becoming an English teacher and match paragraph headings 1–4 with paragraphs A–D.

1 Working hours   **2** Holidays   **3** Location
4 Responsibilities

A guide to ... becoming an English teacher

Are you creative and social? Do you enjoy travel and adventure? Do you love language and communicating with people? Then maybe you should be an English teacher!

A ....

You can work in the UK or you can work in another part of the world. A lot of teachers choose to work in another country and this is a great way to see the world. You can work for a school and give English classes there. You can also work for yourself and teach private classes. Some teachers work from home and teach their lessons online.

B ....

Teachers work long hours. They usually have a lot of classes and they want their students to be happy and interested. That's why they spend a lot of time planning their lessons. Teachers work late and often at the weekends, too. In some countries, they work seven days a week! But if you enjoy being creative, then planning lessons is fun!

C ....

You need to be organised because a teacher does a lot of paperwork. You need to check homework and write tests. You have to plan lessons and create fun activities so your students are interested. If you teach children, you have to look after them and also write reports. You should enjoy working with people, too, because you will be working with other teachers, managers, parents and students.

D ....

You can take long holidays if you teach English. Teachers usually have two to three months' holiday every year. They work very hard. That's why they need so much time to relax!

2 Read the text again. Are the sentences true (T) or false (F)?

1 You need to travel to another country to teach English. ....

2 English teachers always work for a company. ....

3 Some teachers don't have a break at the weekend. ....

4 Lesson planning can be fun. ....

5 A teacher needs to be organised because of lesson planning. ....

6 Teachers need to have a lot of holidays because they work hard. ....

3 Read the Focus box. Then find an example of each linker in the guide in Exercise 1.

Linking ideas

When we write, we join two ideas or sentences together with linkers.

To add information, use *and, also* and *too*.

*Teachers work late **and** at the weekends, **too**.*

To give opposite or surprising information, use *but* and *however*. To give a choice, use *or*.

*English teaching doesn't pay well, **but** that's not why we do it!*

*You can work in the UK **or** you can work in another part of the world.*

To give reasons or results, use *because (of), so* and *that's why*.

*You need to be organised **because** a teacher does a lot of paper work.*

*You have to plan lessons and create fun activities **so** your students are interested.*

*They work very hard. **That's why** they need so much time to relax!*

---

4 Choose the correct alternatives.

A life after teaching?

After you teach English for a few years, you might decide that you love it **¹***and*/*but* you want to do it forever. A lot of people make this choice. **²***Also*/*However*, you might want to use your experience in a different job. You could write a coursebook **³***or*/*also* a workbook. You could **⁴***too*/*also* become an editor. Teachers are usually good at working with people. **⁵***However*/*That's why*, you might become a manager. You could start your own school, **⁶***too*/*so*.

Prepare

5 You're going to write a guide about a job that you know well. Look at the headings in the guide in Exercise 1 and make notes for each one.

Write

6 Write your guide. Use your notes in Exercise 5 and the Focus box to help you.

Vocabulary

Happiness

1 **Choose the correct alternatives.**

Stella

When I was a child, my parents spent a lot of time with me and my sister. We had a really happy ¹*friends/family* life. My parents both had ²*good/healthy* careers, but we weren't a rich family. We had a small house and only a little garden. It was a ³*humour/simple* life. When I leave university and get a job, I want my life to be the same.

Richard

When I finish university, the first thing I'll do is look for a job so I can ⁴*keep/earn* lots of money. My career is very important to me, so I will work hard. I don't ⁵*get/have* a lot of interests, so I don't need to have a lot of ⁶*free/simple* time.

Laura

When I leave university, I would like to work in a gym. I think it's important for people to keep ⁷*simple/fit*. I can help them to eat ⁸*well/good* and have healthy lives.

2 **Match the phrases in bold in sentences 1–8 with definitions a–h below.**

1 My best friend and I always make each other laugh. We have the same **sense of humour**! ....

2 We eat a lot of fruit and vegetables because it's important to **eat well**. ....

3 I try not to spend too much time at work. I want to have time for **a happy family life**. ....

4 I have **a busy social life**. My diary is always full! ....

5 Life is better if you **have a lot of interests**. ....

6 My friend wants to start a family soon. I want to have **a good career** before I start a family. ....

7 She goes to the gym three times a week to **keep fit**. ....

8 When he gets a job, he wants to **earn lots of money** so that he can buy lots of things. ....

a spending lots of time with friends
b work you do successfully for many years
c enjoy doing many different things
d eat good food that helps you be healthy
e do physical activities to stay healthy
f being able to laugh at funny things
g enjoying time with your family
h getting paid a lot of money from your job

Grammar

will for predictions

3 **Put the words in brackets in the correct place to complete the predictions.**

In the future, …

    won't

1 people/have telephones in their houses. (won't)

2 people will healthier because of new sports technology. (be)

3 I don't people will use paper money. (think)

4 I think people only use public transport. (will)

5 people will more free time. (have)

6 I think we travel more. ('ll)

7 won't eat so much meat. (people)

8 I think people will drive to work. (don't)

4 **Complete the sentences with *will* or *won't* and the verbs in brackets.**

1 I don't want to go to the party alone. It .... (be) fun on my own.

2 I need to save some money for my holiday. It .... (be) expensive.

3 We need to recycle our plastic or the problem .... (get) worse.

4 I don't want to watch that film. I don't think I .... (enjoy) it.

5 I won't take my umbrella because I don't think it .... (rain) later.

6 You shouldn't eat so much fast food. You .... (stay) healthy.

7 The transport in Paris is great. You .... (have) problems travelling.

5 **Correct the mistake in each prediction.**

    will work

1 People/will to work longer hours.

2 People no will work in offices.

3 I think will it be hard to relax at the weekends.

4 It'll being more difficult to find a job.

5 I think people will doing more than one job.

6 I no think we'll have much free time.

7 People willn't spend a lot of time with their families.

Vocabulary

make, do, have

1 Complete the phrases with *make, do* or *have*.

1 .... an appointment
2 .... a day off
3 .... an excuse
4 .... a cake
5 .... a meeting
6 .... (some) cooking
7 .... lunch
8 .... (some) shopping
9 .... a haircut
10 .... (some) housework
11 .... a meal
12 .... (some) exercise
13 .... a barbecue/picnic
14 .... (some) work

2 Match the sentence halves.

1 Sorry, I can't go out tonight. I have to do _____*i*_____
2 It's my party tomorrow, so I want to help my mother do _____
3 There's nothing in the fridge! I need to go out and do _____
4 I was really tired, so I made _____
5 I have a job interview next week. I think I need to have _____
6 My house is such a mess, but I hate doing _____
7 It's a beautiful day. Let's go to the park and have _____
8 I can't decide what to have _____
9 I want to get fit. I need to do _____
10 It's Clare's birthday next week. I want to make _____

a an excuse and left the party early.
b housework. It's boring!
c a picnic and play games.
d more exercise.
e some shopping or I will be hungry!
f some cooking for it.
g a haircut before then.
h a cake to celebrate.
i some work before my presentation tomorrow.
j for lunch today.

Grammar

Present continuous for future arrangements

3 Put the words in the correct order to make questions.

1 Monday / you / Who / are / with / having / lunch / on / ?
....
2 What / on / evening / doing / are / Friday / you / ?
....
3 Are / you / the / office / in / working / on / Tuesday / ?
....
4 going / When / the / are / gym / you / to / ?
....
5 How / yoga / many / this / are / times / you / doing / week / ?
....
6 dinner / mum / When / meeting / your / are / you / for / ?
....
7 are / going / cinema / you / Who / to / the / with / ?
....
8 on / Are / you / Thursday / doing / anything / ?
....

4 Look at the diary. Then answer the questions in Exercise 3 using the present continuous.

Monday	Tuesday	Wednesday	Thursday	Friday
06.30 do yoga	07.00 travel to Birmingham	06.30 do yoga	have a day off	
13.30–15.00 have lunch with Chris				12.30 go to the gym
19.00–23.00 go to the cinema with Sarah		19.00 meet Mum for dinner		20.00 fly to Rome

1 *I'm having lunch with Chris on Monday.*
2 ....
3 ....
4 ....
5 ....
6 ....
7 ....
8 ....

5 Complete the sentences with the correct form of the verbs in the box.

cook   ~~do~~   go   have   leave   meet   play   start

1 What _____*are*_____ you _____*doing*_____ tomorrow night?
2 We .... on holiday a week on Friday.
3 I .... a new course in June.
4 I .... not .... dinner tonight. We're going to a restaurant.
5 Hurry up! The train .... in five minutes!
6 They .... an important meeting on 24th May.
7 We .... tennis three times next week.
8 Where .... you .... Paul tonight?

6c

Vocabulary

Weekend activities

1 Complete the table with the words and phrases in the box.

~~activities~~   cycling   dancing/clubbing
gardening   homework   in a band
nothing   shopping   swimming
video games   volleyball   yoga

do	go	play
activities		

2 Complete the sentences with the words in the box.

activities   do   go   going   nothing
playing   plays   running
video games   yoga

1 I love .... swimming in the sea when I'm on holiday.
2 Did you have to .... much homework when you were at school?
3 My friend Rob .... the guitar in a band.
4 I often .... shopping with my mum on Saturdays.
5 I love doing .... on Sundays. I sometimes stay in bed all day!
6 How often do you .... dancing at the weekend?
7 My friend Kim does .... every day – she's very fit!
8 I love playing .... with my friends. I usually win!
9 I do lots of .... in my free time. I like to keep busy.
10 I'm really tired because I went .... at six o'clock this morning.

Grammar

may and might

3 Put the words in brackets in the correct place to complete the sentences.

                                          might
1 You shouldn't order too much food because you⁄not finish it! (might)

2 I didn't study very hard, so I might pass the exam. (not)

3 When I leave university, I do some travelling. (might)

4 I want to do some exercise this weekend, but I not have enough time. (may)

5 It's going to be sunny tomorrow, so I might some gardening. (do)

6 My back is hurting a lot, so I go to the doctor. (might)

7 I want to see the new horror film, but my friends may want to. (not)

8 I might a barbecue this weekend. (have)

4 Complete the sentences with the positive or negative form of the words in brackets.

1 I _might not_ (might) go out tonight, I'm quite tired.
2 I .... (might) go for a walk later if I finish work early.
3 English grammar is quite difficult, but this book .... (may) help me.
4 Let's get there early because there .... (may) be a long queue.
5 I don't think we should watch that film. We .... (may) enjoy it.
6 I want to get fit, so I .... (might) try a yoga class at the new gym.
7 We have theatre tickets for this evening, but we .... (might) go.
8 The weather looks OK now, but it .... (may) rain later.

5 Rewrite the sentences. Replace the underlined words with may/might (not).

1 <u>Maybe</u> I <u>will</u> see you later.
   I might see you later.
2 <u>It's possible that</u> I <u>won't</u> have time to see you today.
   ....
3 <u>Maybe</u> it <u>won't</u> rain tomorrow.
   ....
4 <u>Perhaps</u> John <u>doesn't</u> like spicy food.
   ....
5 <u>It's possible that</u> I <u>will</u> do some cooking tonight.
   ....
6 <u>Maybe</u> the shop <u>will</u> be open late tomorrow.
   ....
7 <u>I am not sure if it's</u> a good idea.
   ....
8 <u>Perhaps</u> I <u>will</u> go dancing this weekend.
   ....

Functional language

Leave a phone message

1 **Put the words in brackets in the correct order to complete the voice messages.**

> Hello. This is Michael Andrews from the hair salon.
> 1 ....
> (a / This / is / for / message / Mrs Davis). I'm really sorry
> 2 ....
> (have / appointment / but / cancel / I / to / your).
> 3 ....
> (back / Call / me / on) this number, and we can make another appointment for next week.

> Hi Jeanne, it's Sarah here.
> 4 ....
> (tell / I'm / to / calling / you) about my date last night! Can you call me 5 ....
> (get / back / this / when / you) ?

> Hello, dear, 6 ....
> (your / is / mother / this).
> 7 ....
> (about / calling / I'm) your sister's party.
> 8 ....
> (Give / a / call / me) when you have time.

> Hi John, it's Mohammed.
> 9 ....
> (I'm / about / to / you / calling / remind) lunch tomorrow. I know you're at work now, but
> 10 ....
> (when / me / you're / text / free).

2 **Complete the voice messages with the verbs in the box.**

> call   calling   cancel   give   is   let   remind

> Hi. This ¹ .... Nora.
> I'm really sorry but I have to ² .... dinner tonight. My son is sick, so I'm staying at home. Please text me to ³ .... me know you got this message.
> Thanks, and sorry!

> Hello. This is a message for Mr Jacobs from Harley Street Dentist's.
> I'm calling to ⁴ .... you about your appointment at 9 a.m. on Tuesday morning. Can you ⁵ .... me back if you need to cancel this appointment?
> Thank you.

> Hi, it's me. I'm ⁶ .... to see how you are.
> I know you're busy at the moment, but ⁷ .... me a call when you have time.
> OK, bye!

Listening

1 🔊 6.01 **Listen to a radio programme about countries with the happiest people. Put the countries in the box in the correct order.**

> Australia   Canada   Norway   Sweden   Switzerland

1st ....
2nd ....
3rd ....
4th ....
5th ....

2 **Listen again. Choose the correct alternatives.**

1 Australia has good *food / weather*.
2 Australians *like / don't like* their government.
3 In Sweden, *schools are / transport is* good.
4 *Ninety / Ninety-two* percent of Swiss people said they were happy.
5 Norway is good for *work / tourists*.
6 Canada is very *clean / safe*.

3a **Complete the sentences with the names of the countries.**

1 .... has very little pollution.
2 Seventy-five percent of people in .... have a job.
3 There is good education in Sweden and in ....
4 People in .... are very healthy.
5 There is good weather in ....
6 Ninety-three percent said they were happy living in ....
7 .... is a safe country to have a family.
8 Crime is very low in ....
9 In .... , many people like their government.
10 .... is a good country for skiing.

b **Listen again and check.**

6

Reading

1 Read the article about how successful people spend their free time. Match headings a–e with paragraphs 1–5.

a They do charity work
b They spend time with friends and family
c They do exercise
d They have hobbies
e They read

2 Read the article again. Are the sentences true (T) or false (F)?

1 To be successful we need to make big changes. ....
2 Reading helps us know more about the world. ....
3 Exercise helps us to not feel stress. ....
4 Successful people have to work all the time. ....
5 Successful people don't work for free. ....
6 Many people usually spend lots of time working. ....

3 Read the article again. Answer the questions.

1 When we read, what can we learn about?

....

2 What does improving your vocabulary help you do?

....

3 How often do successful people do exercise?

....

4 How can exercise help us?

....

5 Which two hobbies does the writer talk about?

....

6 How can hobbies help us with work?

....

7 What can successful people do to help the local community?

....

8 Why do successful people sometimes work for free?

....

9 What happens if we only think about ourselves and our work?

....

10 What is as important as time at work?

....

4 Find words in the text to match definitions 1–5.

1 make better (paragraph 1) ....
2 often (paragraph 2) ....
3 a short rest from work (paragraph 3) ....
4 the people in the area where you live (paragraph 4)
....
5 unhappy because you are not with other people (paragraph 5) ....

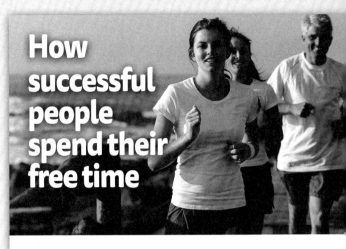

How successful people spend their free time

When you finish a busy day at work, what do you do? Do you go home and play computer games or watch films? This is not what successful people do! Read about five different ways successful people spend their free time. These small things could change your life!

1 ....

Books help us understand the world. This is why successful people read a lot of them! When successful people read, they learn about new cultures and environments. This helps them get new ideas and learn to think in a different way. Reading also helps us improve our vocabulary, so we can communicate better with people around us.

2 ....

Physical activity is good for everyone, and successful people do this regularly. If we go swimming, go running or go to the gym, we get stronger and healthier. A good exercise routine also helps us to not feel stressed. It makes us feel good and look good. Successful people do exercise at least three times every week.

3 ....

You might think that successful people have to work all the time, but this is not true. Successful people enjoy improving their skills in other areas, too. A hobby can make us happy and it gives us a break from work. Playing guitar in a band, learning how to dance or doing other kinds of activities can help us to relax. Hobbies can help us feel ready to start work the next day, with new ideas.

4 ....

Successful people often want to help the local community. For example, they give money to places that help poor people or they give a job to someone who needs one. Sometimes they work for free because it makes them feel happy. They think this is a good way to give something back to other people.

5 ....

For many people, it's normal to spend a lot of time at work. A job is important, but it isn't everything in life. Successful people know that spending time with friends and family is really important, too. We should go for dinner with friends or watch a film with our families. People can feel sad and lonely if they only think about themselves and their work. Our time with friends and family is as important as our time at work.

6

Writing

1 Read Michelle's blog post. What is her problem?

1 I'm so busy at the moment and I don't know when it's going to stop! I'm taking extra classes at university and I have so much to do. My calendar is too full and I'm stressed!

2 The last few weeks have been very difficult. I had to do a lot of housework because my parents came to visit me. They left yesterday and I'm happy they came, but now I'm behind with my studies!

3 Next week will also be very busy! On Wednesday I'm taking an exam and then on Thursday morning I have to meet my teacher to talk about the results. My best friend, Claire, is having a party on Friday, so I need to buy her present Friday afternoon.

4 I know people say it's good to be busy, but everyday life is difficult right now and I need help! I need to organise my time better because right now I don't have any free time!

2 Read the text again. Answer the questions.
1 Where does Michelle study?

2 Why is she stressed?

3 Why did she do a lot of housework last week?

4 Why is she going to meet her teacher?

5 What is happening on Friday?

6 How can Michelle improve her situation?

3a Read the sentences about how to organise your writing. Choose the correct alternatives.
1 It's better to write *in one long text / using paragraphs*.
2 When you use paragraphs, your ideas are *clearer / more interesting*.
3 Each paragraph usually has *one main idea / two main ideas*.
4 The first sentence in a paragraph usually *introduces the topic / gives details*.
5 The other sentences in a paragraph often *introduce new ideas / give details*.

b Read the Focus box and check your ideas.

Organising ideas in paragraphs

Organise and write information in paragraphs so the reader can follow it more easily. Each paragraph usually has one topic or main idea.
The first sentence often introduces the topic or main idea. The other sentences give more details.
I'm so busy at the moment and I don't know when it's going to stop! *I'm taking extra classes at university and have so much to do. My calendar is too full!*

4 Read the blog post in Exercise 1 again. Choose the main idea for each paragraph from the phrases in the box.

being busy can make life hard   being busy is good
I'm always busy   I'm really busy right now
I was more relaxed last month   next week is the same
next week looks better
the last few weeks were busy, too

Paragraph 1

Paragraph 2

Paragraph 3

Paragraph 4

Prepare

5 You're going to write a blog post about how busy you are at the moment. First, make notes about the questions below.
1 How busy is your life at the moment? What things are you doing?
2 What were the last few weeks like? What things did you do?
3 What are your plans for this week and the next few weeks?
4 Do you want to be busier or less busy? Why?

Write

6 Write your blog post. Organise the information in paragraphs. Use your notes in Exercise 5 and the Focus box to help you.

Vocabulary

Features of city life

1 **Choose the correct alternatives.**

1 This is a great *area/local* to live in. There are lots of good schools and shops nearby.

2 It's dangerous to ride a bike in the city centre because there aren't any *cycle/bike* paths.

3 They're building some new *flats/areas* in the town centre.

4 The flat's in a really *good/right* location, next to the park.

5 I buy bread and milk from the *local/near* shop.

6 I met my new *neighbours/people* yesterday – they've moved into the flat next to mine.

7 I love living in a big city – the *nightlife/daylife* is great!

8 It's noisy here because of all the *traffic/pollution*.

2 **Complete the sentences with the words in the box.**

area   cycle paths   flat   local   location   neighbours
nightlife   pollution   public transport   traffic

1 Our city needs a better .... system, to help people travel.

2 It's easy to travel by bike in our town because we have a lot of ....

3 There's a lot of traffic in our city and the .... is really bad.

4 It's sad that a lot of .... shops closed when the big supermarket opened in our town.

5 Yesterday, new .... moved into the house next door.

6 Gemma has lived in this .... for ten years. She really enjoys living here.

7 The house is in a good .... because it's close to my daughter's school.

8 My .... is on the fourth floor of the building.

9 This area is popular with students because the .... is great.

10 I don't want to drive into town because there's a lot of ....

Grammar

too and *enough*

3 **Choose the correct alternatives.**

1 **A:** Can you make everyone some tea, please?
   B: I'm sorry, there aren't *enough/too many* tea bags.

2 **A:** Did you buy that shirt you liked in the shop?
   B: No, I didn't, because it was *too/too much* small.

3 **A:** Are you finished and ready to go home?
   B: I can't because I have *enough/too much* work to do.

4 **A:** Can I pack my things in your suitcase?
   B: No, you can't, because I have too *much/many* clothes.

5 **A:** Can you carry this heavy box?
   B: No, I can't, because I'm not *strong enough/ enough strong*.

6 **A:** Did you go to the concert last night?
   B: No, I didn't, because I was *too busy/busy too*.

7 **A:** Are you going on holiday this summer?
   B: No, I'm not, because I don't have *money enough/ enough money*.

8 **A:** Are you happy with your hotel room?
   B: No, we're not, because it's *not clean enough/ too much clean*.

4 **Complete the sentences with *too, too many* or *too much*.**

1 There are .... people on this bus. It's very crowded!

2 The things in this shop are .... expensive. Let's go to another shop.

3 I made .... mistakes, so I failed my driving test.

4 I can't study because there's .... noise!

5 I hope the film isn't .... long because I want to go to bed early.

6 I feel that there's .... work and that I will never finish it!

7 It's difficult to cycle on the roads because there are .... cars.

8 I think it's .... far to walk and that we should get a taxi.

5 **Correct the mistake in each sentence.**

1 Do you think the house is enough big for us?

2 Holly says there is food enough for the party.

3 There aren't enough time for us to catch the train.

4 Many cities don't have enough spaces big.

5 Those jeans aren't enough long for your legs!

6 Do we haven't enough food for everyone?

Vocabulary

Natural features

1 **Complete the sentences with the words in the box.**

beach   forest   hill   mountain   ocean   river
stream   wood

1 One day, I want to climb a _____ in the Himalayas.
2 There's a huge _____ near my house. I love walking there among all the trees, but it's easy to get lost.
3 When I was a child, I used to jump over the little _____ at the end of our garden.
4 Sometimes I go fishing with my dad. We don't live near the sea, so we go to a nearby _____ .
5 I want to sail across the _____ in my new boat!
6 Let's go on holiday to Greece. We can relax on the _____ and enjoy the sunshine.
7 There's a small _____ behind my house. The trees are beautiful and there are lots of interesting birds and insects.
8 We went for a walk in the countryside today and climbed a big _____ . It took us half an hour!

2 **Choose the correct alternatives.**

1 We spent our holiday on the *forest/beach* and lay in the sun.
2 In the Maldives, you can sometimes see whales in the *ocean/stream*.
3 There are so many trees in this *forest/lake*! It will be easy to get lost!
4 Our house is at the top of the *hill/wood*.
5 This *lake/stream* runs through the valley into the river.
6 We love going boating on the *ocean/lake* in the park.
7 It took me five days to climb the *mountain/hill*.
8 You can swim in the *sea/beach* all year because it's always warm.
9 The elephants visit the *river/forest* every night to drink water.
10 Let's go for a walk in the *hill/wood*. I love the smell of the trees at this time of year.

Grammar

used to

3 **Choose the correct alternatives.**

1 Before he lived in the city, Noah *used to/use to* live with his family on a farm.
2 We *didn't use to/used to* listen to classical music, but now we love it!
3 Frank *use to/used to* think school was difficult and he was quite unhappy.
4 Did you *used to/use to* cycle to work every day?
5 Roger *didn't use to/didn't used to* cook at all, but now he tries new recipes every day.
6 Did Sue and Fred *used to/use to* live in the Bahamas?
7 I *didn't use to/used to* go to the gym every day, but I'm too busy now.
8 My grandmother *used to/didn't use to* like walking in the woods because she loved doing exercise.

4 **Rewrite the sentences using *used to, didn't use to* or *did ... use to.***

1 As a child, I lived near the sea.
   As a child, I used to live near the sea.
2 Did you ever swim in the lake when you were young?
   _____
3 My brother had purple hair and a big beard.
   _____
4 We were really good friends, but now we don't speak at all.
   _____
5 Did Crystal work for your family?
   _____
6 The giraffes didn't come into the forest before.
   _____
7 We wrote letters, but now we only write emails.
   _____
8 I didn't enjoy cooking, but now I love it.
   _____

5 **Correct the mistake in each sentence.**

1 Did you used to cycle to school or get the bus?
2 My teachers used to shouting at me when I didn't do my homework.
3 My brother didn't use eat green vegetables. It made my mum really angry.
4 What did you use to doing before you started work here?
5 I use to know lots of people in my neighbourhood, but they've moved away now.
6 When I was at school, we used do a big test every week.
7 Nick don't use to enjoy his job, but now he loves it!
8 Sam be used to less fit than she is now.

Vocabulary

Prepositions

1 **Choose the correct option a, b or c.**

1 When you arrive, please put your bags _____ the corner of the room.

   a on   b in   c at

2 The post office is _____ the bank, so you need to cross the road.

   a opposite   b on   c between

3 Put your pencil _____ your desk when you finish the exam.

   a behind   b under   c on

4 I was waiting _____ the cinema for ages, but you didn't come.

   a under   b in front of   c between

5 Many old cities have tunnels _____ their streets.

   a on   b under   c behind

6 We used to live _____ each other at university.

   a on   b behind   c next to

7 There's a beautiful old lamp _____ the room.

   a at   b behind   c in the corner of

8 You can't see it, but _____ that big building is a small lake.

   a behind   b under   c in the corner

9 Your bag is where you left it – _____ the bed and the wardrobe.

   a on   b in the middle   c between

10 There's a small botanical garden _____ the train station, which is very unusual.

   a between   b in the middle of   c under

2 **Complete the sentences with the words in the box.**

> behind   between   in front of   in the corner   in the middle of
> next to   on   ~~opposite~~   under

1 The house is _opposite_ the cathedral, so we have a great view of it.

2 Can you all sit _____ each other in a circle?

3 We keep our suitcases _____ top of the wardrobe.

4 The cat was hiding _____ the sofa because it was scared.

5 Have you seen the new statue _____ the square?

6 During the race, I tried to get _____ the others, but they were too fast.

7 The train stopped _____ two stations for a long time.

8 You'll find the new clothes lines _____ of the shop.

9 I like to sit _____ the big tree in the garden when it's very sunny.

Grammar

Articles

3 **Choose the correct alternatives.**

1 There's *a/the* new film at the cinema. Do you want to see it this weekend?

2 We can buy *–/a* flowers for your aunt at the station.

3 I lost *the/a* new jumper I told you about yesterday.

4 I need to get *an/–* appointment at the dentist today because my tooth really hurts!

5 There's *a/an* cash machine next to the tourist information office.

6 Lots of *–/the* people are very worried about the environment.

7 I enjoy listening to *the/–* music with my friends.

8 They built a new house on *a/the* corner of our street.

9 Our home has *a/–* large garden with lots of trees.

10 I like to have a lot of *–/the* space at home.

4 **Complete the conversations with *a*, *an*, *the* or no article (–).**

1 A: Hi, Aaron. Did you know our neighbour has got _____ new dog?

   B: Hello, Beci. No, I didn't know about _____ dog. Oh dear! I don't like _____ animals.

   A: Oh! I didn't know that. _____ dog is really well trained, so I don't think it will be a problem.

2 A: Hi, Georgia. Tell me all about your new flat.

   B: Hi, Miriam! I really love my new flat. There's _____ big garden and lots of _____ space outside.

   A: Oh, wow! How many _____ rooms has it got?

   B: There are _____ four rooms and _____ big bathroom. _____ bathroom has _____ amazing shower!

3 A: Hello, Bella. How was _____ party last weekend?

   B: Oh, it was great. My mum baked me _____ huge cake.

   A: Really! I love _____ birthday cakes. Did lots of _____ people come to your party?

   B: Oh, yes. Lots of my friends came, but I missed you, of course!

Functional language

Make and respond to excuses

1 Put the words in the correct order to make sentences.

1 really / I'm / sorry / late / I'm

2 money / I don't / I'm / have / sorry / enough

3 afraid / I'm / didn't / I / computer / me / my / bring / with

4 I / meet / you / I'm / sorry / later / busy / so / can't

5 can't / sorry / book club / come / can't / tonight / I / to

2 Choose the correct alternatives.

a It doesn't *matter/worry*. I can pay for the tickets.

b No *problem/mind*. I can tell you all about it tomorrow.

c Never *matter/mind*. How about tomorrow night instead?

d Don't *worry/worries* about it. We've got enough time.

e That's all *right/matter*. We can write in our notebooks.

3 Match responses a–e in Exercise 2 with sentences 1–5 in Exercise 1.

1 _____ 2 _____ 3 _____ 4 _____ 5 _____

4 Complete the conversations with the words in the box.

afraid can't matter never really sorry
worries worry

1 **A:** Morning Kate.
B: Hi Jane. I'm really _____ but I have to work late today, so I can't come for a drink after work later.
A: Don't _____ about it. I'm quite tired, so I'll probably go straight home.

2 **A:** Hi Jonathan. Is everything OK?
B: Hey Andy. Um ... I'm _____ I forgot to bring your birthday present.
A: It doesn't _____ – I'm just happy to see you!

3 **A:** Hi there. Do you want to come to an art exhibition with me on Saturday?
B: Sorry, I _____ . I'm going on holiday on Friday.
A: _____ mind. Next time!

4 **A:** I'm _____ sorry but I think I have broken your TV remote control.
B: No _____ . It's probably just the battery!

Listening

1 🔊 7.01 Listen to a meeting about a graffiti project. Does everyone in the meeting think the project is a good idea?

2 Listen again. Are the sentences true (T) or false (F)?

1 The graffiti art project is for a city. _____
2 There is graffiti in Berlin. _____
3 Elisabeth is from London. _____
4 There are art students at the local college. _____
5 Tony and Elisabeth agree with each other. _____
6 Graffiti is art which is in the streets. _____
7 Graffiti art can have a lot of colour. _____
8 There won't be a vote to decide about the project. _____

3a Choose the correct alternatives.

1 Tony *lives/doesn't live* in the town.
2 Elisabeth *likes/doesn't like* the idea of graffiti.
3 Elisabeth says that graffiti *is/isn't* art.
4 Tony says that graffiti is *a different kind of art from/the same kind of art as* Francis Bacon.
5 Tony believes that the art students *can/can't* create interesting art.
6 Elisabeth is worried that *more/fewer* tourists will visit the town.
7 The woman says that graffiti *will/won't* bring colour to the streets.
8 The man says that we *know/don't know* if other young people can do graffiti well.

b Listen again and check.

Reading

1 **Read the article about life on a canal boat. Choose the best title a, b or c.**

   a Why everyone should live on a boat

   b How to live on a boat

   c Why you shouldn't buy a boat

2 **Read the article again. Are the sentences true (T) or false (F)?**

   1 Not many people think boat life is a good idea. ....

   2 Real life on a boat is not the same as the idea. ....

   3 The weather is good for most of the year. ....

   4 You can sail your boat very quickly on the canals. ....

   5 No one can stay in one place for longer than two weeks. ....

   6 It's difficult to find a place to buy a boat. ....

   7 It can cost £25,000 or more to buy a canal boat. ....

   8 Life on a boat is twice as cheap as life in a house or flat. ....

3 **Read the article again. Answer the questions.**

   1 Why is life on a boat attractive?

   2 What's the problem for half the year when you live on a boat?

   3 What rule do you need to follow when you're travelling on a boat?

   4 What does the writer say is difficult in paragraph 3?

   5 What's the problem with staying in one place all the time?

   6 Why can it be better to buy an old boat?

   7 How much cheaper can it be living in a boat than a flat or house?

   8 What do you need to do if things break?

4 **Find words in the text with the opposite meaning to words 1–6. The first letter is given.**

   1 noisy – q............ (paragraph 1)

   2 grey – c............ (paragraph 1)

   3 ugly – b............ (paragraph 2)

   4 cheap – e............ (paragraph 3)

   5 save – s............ (paragraph 5)

   6 break – f............ (paragraph 6)

Why do people live on canal boats?

I think a lot of people like the idea. They think of a boat sailing on quiet waters. The canals are green with trees and nature, and the other boats are very colourful. Also, people feel free when they are in a boat. You can be your own captain and go anywhere you want. You travel in your own home! In London, there are over 100 miles of canals.

What is it really like?

I think people quickly understand that real life on a canal boat is very different from the idea! Yes, things can be beautiful, but for more than half the year it can be cold and wet. You have very little space in the boat. You might find it difficult if you like a lot of space. You get a lot of freedom in a boat, but there are also lots of rules you need to follow. For example, you can only travel at four miles per hour. The best thing is the other people you meet who also live on boats. They're amazing!

How long can you stay in one place?

Boats can stay in most places on the canal. The good news is that it's free! But the rule is that you have to move your boat every two weeks. This can be quite difficult and some people don't want to move so much. You can pay to stay in one place, but this can be very expensive.

How can you buy a boat?

Lots of companies sell boats. You can even pay someone to design and build a boat for you. It's not a good idea to buy a new boat to begin with. You might not like boat life. It can be better to buy an old boat.

How much does it cost?

You can spend less if you live on a boat than if you live in a flat or house. First you need to buy the boat, which can cost between £25,000 and £75,000. You also need to pay for a boat licence, which can be £500. But after that, your costs should be about 70–80 percent less than for a flat or house.

Do you need special training?

No, you don't need special training. But you do need to understand your boat and how it works. You will want to be able to fix things when they break!

Writing

1 Read the email. Why is Johnny writing to Pete?

● ● ●

From:	petepiper@giggle.com
To:	johnnyjjones@kgmail.co.us
Subject:	Holiday plans

Hi Pete,

Great to hear from you. Everything's fine here. We're enjoying lots of sunshine. The sun is always shining here in California! We spend the weekends at the beach or in the garden. It's great!

It was very interesting to get your news. Sophie's new job sounds fantastic! We'd love to hear more about it. What does she think of her new office? Does she like her new colleagues?

Anyway, I'm writing to find out if we can come and visit you in August. We haven't seen you for more than two years now, and we need to catch up with all your news. We'd like to spend some time in London as well. Maybe we can meet up with our old university friends there?

Talk with Sophie and let me know what you think!

Bye for now,

Johnny

2 Read the email again. Choose the correct alternatives.

1 Johnny and Pete live in the *same country/ different countries.*

2 Johnny spends a lot of time *inside/outside* because of the weather.

3 Sophie has been working in her job for a *short/long* time.

4 Johnny *wants/doesn't want* to have a holiday in August.

5 Johnny wants to visit the *UK/US.*

6 Pete *lives/doesn't live* in London.

3 Read the Focus box. Which informal phrases in the box does Johnny use in his email?

Informal phrases

When writing emails to friends and family, there are some specific phrases that you can use to make the message sound friendly.

Saying how you are

Everything's fine here.   I'm fine.

Responding/Asking how someone is

*Great to hear from you.   Lovely to get your email.
How are things?*

Responding to/Asking about news

*I can't believe …   It sounds fantastic!
How's your new job going?*

Ending an email

Take care.   Bye for now.

4 Complete the sentences with the words in the box.

> bye   can't   hear   is   sounds   take   things

1 Hi there, how are _____ with you?

2 The festival you wrote about _____ fantastic. Let's go together!

3 Let's speak soon. _____ care.

4 Don't worry about us, everything _____ fine here.

5 I _____ believe you've got a new puppy!

6 It's been a long time, and it's really great to _____ from you again.

7 Let's meet on Sunday. _____ for now.

Prepare

5 You're going to write an email to a friend or family member to give them your news and plan to visit them. First, make notes about the questions below.

- What is your news?
- What news would you like to ask about?
- What is your plan to visit them?

Write

6 Write your email. Use your notes in Exercise 5 and the Focus box to help you.

Grammar

Past continuous

1 **Choose the correct alternatives.**

1 While I *sat/was sitting* at my desk, a football *came/was coming* through my window!

2 I *looked/was looking* out of my window when I *saw/was seeing* a fox in my garden.

3 I *fell over/was falling over* on the ice while I *walked/was walking* home.

4 While I *ate/was eating* my lunch, I *heard/was hearing* a loud noise.

5 I *saw/was seeing* you earlier when I *shopped/was shopping*.

6 When I *came/was coming* home, he *watched/was watching* TV.

7 She *met/was meeting* her boyfriend while she *travelled/was travelling* around South America.

8 When I first *saw/was seeing* you, you *wore/were wearing* a beautiful dress.

2 **Complete the sentences with the past simple or past continuous form of the verbs in brackets.**

1 I _____ (not go) to the gym yesterday.

2 I _____ (eat) too much yesterday.

3 Sorry, could you repeat that? I _____ (not listen).

4 When I went out, it _____ (rain).

5 My neighbours _____ (argue) when I came home last night.

6 I _____ (injure) my leg while I was playing football.

7 I _____ (not enjoy) the film because some people were talking too loudly.

8 I saw a mouse while I _____ (clean) the house!

9 He _____ (not play) video games last night because he had too much homework.

10 I took some amazing photos while I _____ (travel) in India.

3 **Complete the sentences with the words in the box.**

> a   ago   days   last   once   week   when   while

1 I fell over _____ few days ago while I was playing tennis.

2 I lost my job _____ month because the company wasn't making money.

3 I _____ found £50 while I was walking in the street.

4 I fell asleep _____ I was reading my book.

5 I was studying a lot a few weeks _____ , but now I've finished my exams.

6 I don't want Chinese food again! We ate it a few _____ ago.

7 I lost my phone last _____ .

8 It was raining _____ we met.

Vocabulary

Verbs of movement

4 **Complete the sentences with the words in the box.**

> around (x2)   back   down   into   out   over   up

1 I arrived late and they didn't let me go _____ the theatre.

2 Last summer, we travelled _____ France and saw lots of places.

3 After he fell off his bike, he got _____ slowly.

4 I went ice skating and didn't fall _____ once!

5 I was bored at home, so I went _____ for a walk.

6 I have a headache. I think I'll go and lie _____ .

7 I heard someone say my name, so I turned _____ .

8 If you are busy, I can come _____ later.

5 **Match the sentence halves.**

1 I locked the door carefully before I went _____

2 I was tired after work, so I lay _____

3 The art exhibition looked interesting, so I went _____

4 My mum was angry because I came _____

5 I heard my name, so I turned _____

6 I've never been to the US, but I've travelled _____

7 When I was a child, I fell _____

8 After the accident at football practice, I got _____

a around most of Europe.

b around to see who was calling me.

c down for a few minutes before dinner.

d back very late last night.

e up slowly because I had a headache.

f out for the evening.

g over a lot and hurt myself!

h into the gallery to see it.

8B

Vocabulary

Transport

1 **Cross out the word that does not go with the verb.**

1 **take** a ferry/train/~~car~~
2 **rent** a car/flight/bike
3 **get out of** a taxi/car/bike
4 **park** a train/bike/car
5 **miss** a bus/car/train
6 **get on** a bike/holiday/tram
7 **get in** a cable car/bus/car
8 **get off** a taxi/bike/plane

2 **Choose the correct alternatives.**

> The worst journey I have had was when I went to Brazil. I was really excited to leave London and discover Rio de Janeiro. Unfortunately, the train to the airport was cancelled, so we **¹**got on/missed our flight and had to wait for the next one. Our plan was to **²**book/rent a car when we arrived in Brazil, but this didn't happen. We arrived at 11 p.m., so the car hire place was closed! We had to **³**take/book a taxi. Luckily, there were lots of taxis **⁴**parked/rented outside the airport. We were so happy when we **⁵**got in/got on the taxi and our driver told us he knew our hotel. Unfortunately, there were a lot of cars on the road, and we got stuck in traffic. After an hour, our driver told us he couldn't continue. We had to **⁶**get out of/get off the taxi and walk! We had all our bags, so this was really difficult. Luckily, after ten minutes we found a tram stop. We **⁷**got in/got on a tram at 12.30 a.m. It was a long journey, but when we **⁸**got out of/got off the tram we were at the hotel!

Grammar

because, so and *to*

3 **Match the sentence halves.**

1 You should walk to work ....
2 You should avoid walking alone late at night ....
3 You should book your hotel for the holiday ....
4 You can rent a car at the airport ....
5 Remember to take a map with you ....
6 You should plan your holiday ....
7 You can travel outside the city ....
8 Try to take a cable car ....

a because it can be dangerous.
b so you don't get lost.
c to save money on transport.
d so you don't need to take public transport.
e because there is a lot to see and do.
f because the views are amazing.
g to see the countryside.
h so you have a reservation.

4 **Complete the travel advice with *because, so* or *to*.**

1 Book your flights early .... save money.
2 Visit cheap countries .... you spend less.
3 Use websites .... find the best prices.
4 Don't travel during school holidays .... it's more expensive.
5 Stay in hostels .... they are cheaper than hotels.
6 Don't buy money at the airport .... it's too expensive.
7 Arrive at the airport early .... you don't miss your flight.
8 Use a travel company .... plan where to go.

5 **Put the words in the correct order to complete the answers.**

1 **A:** Why were you late?
  B: I was late ....
  (car / because / broke / my / down)
2 **A:** Why did you take a taxi?
  B: I took a taxi ....
  (late / wouldn't / so / I / be)
3 **A:** Why did you go to Paris?
  B: I went to Paris ....
  (visit / to / an / friend / old)
4 **A:** Why are you crying?
  B: I'm crying ....
  (view / is / beautiful / the / because)
5 **A:** Why are you going out?
  B: I'm going out ....
  (to / dinner / some / buy / food / for)
6 **A:** Why do you walk everywhere?
  B: I walk everywhere ....
  (stay / can / I / so / healthy)

Vocabulary

Travel

1 **Complete the sentences with the words in the box.**

> alone   book   cruise   pack   plan   shopping   sightseeing   tour   trying

1 When I go on holiday I love _____ new things. Last year I went sailing!
2 We went _____ in Paris. The first thing we saw was the Eiffel Tower of course!
3 My dad's going on an organised _____ of the city. It's good because he always gets lost by himself!
4 I really need to _____ my trip – I'm leaving in two weeks!
5 I'm only going away for two days, so I'll just _____ a small bag.
6 I need to _____ a hotel in London. Can you recommend a good one?
7 I like travelling _____ so I can listen to music and read my book.
8 My parents went on a Mediterranean _____ – they said there were five restaurants on the ship!
9 We went _____ in Tokyo and spent too much money!

2 **Choose the correct alternatives.**

A: I should ¹*pack/plan* my bags. I have a flight tomorrow.
B: Really? Where are you going?
A: I'm ²*going/going on* holiday!
B: Great! Where are you going?
A: Sardinia, in Italy. I ³*booked/planned* my flight six months ago!
B: That sounds lovely. Will it be your first time in Sardinia?
A: Yes, but I'm ⁴*travelling/trying* alone, so I'm a little bit worried.
B: I'm sure you'll be OK.
A: Thanks. I'm ⁵*travelling/going* on an organised tour so I can see the best parts.
B: Wonderful! I went there a few years ago. It's a beautiful country.
A: I'm so excited! I want to relax, eat good food and ⁶*go/go on* shopping!

Grammar

Verb patterns

3 **Choose the correct alternatives.**

1 I *don't mind/want* travelling by coach.
2 He *loves/would like* to visit the museum.
3 We *want/don't mind* to swim in the sea.
4 I *love/would like* going on city tours.
5 They *want/hate* paying a lot for taxis.
6 What do you *want/enjoy* to do on holiday this summer?

4 **Complete the questions with the correct form of the verbs in brackets.**

1 Would you like _____ (go) on an organised tour?
2 Do you want _____ (plan) a trip to Spain?
3 Do you enjoy _____ (travel) alone?
4 Don't you hate _____ (pack) your suitcase before a holiday?
5 Do you love _____ (try) new things on holiday?
6 Would you like _____ (go) into town for dinner?

5 **Write the second sentence so it has a similar meaning to the first. Use the words in brackets.**

1 I'd like to try some local food. (want)
   I want to try some local food.
2 I like renting a bike on holiday. (enjoy)
   _____
3 I hate travelling by boat. It makes me feel sick. (don't want)
   _____
4 Staying in a hostel is OK with me. (don't mind)
   _____
5 I want to go to the beach tomorrow. (would like)
   _____
6 I really like going on cruises. (love)
   _____

Functional language

Give directions

1 Choose the correct option a, b or c.

1 At the roundabout, _____ left.

   a turn   b straight   c take

2 You'll _____ a big cinema on the right.

   a look   b see   c watch

3 It's on _____ left, next to the bank.

   a turn   b the   c take

4 The park is _____ the hotel.

   a in front   b opposite   c on top

5 _____ straight on at the traffic lights.

   a Be   b Take   c Go

6 After the cinema, _____ the third left.

   a take   b go   c walk

7 The police station is at the _____ of the road.

   a left   b opposite   c end

8 The museum is _____ to the park.

   a next   b right   c opposite

2 Complete the conversations with *on*, *at* or *to*.

1 **A:** I'm looking for the main train station. Can you help me?

  B: Sure. Go straight _____ past the station. _____ the roundabout, turn left. You'll see it _____ the left. It's next _____ a big supermarket.

  A: Great, thanks!

2 **A:** I'm lost! I need to get to the library.

  B: Go straight _____ past the park. The police station is _____ the right. Then take the fourth road _____ the left. You'll find the library _____ the end of the road.

3 **A:** Can you tell me how to get to Oliver's Books, please?

  B: Oh yes, I know it. Turn left _____ the hospital. Go straight _____ for about 300 metres. You'll see a big supermarket _____ the right. Oliver's Books is opposite the supermarket.

4 **A:** Excuse me, I'm looking for the shopping mall. It used to be right here, _____ the left!

  B: Yes, it's moved. Don't worry, it's easy to find. _____ the next roundabout, take the third exit. Then take the second road _____ the left. You'll see a big fire station and the shopping mall is next _____ the fire station.

Listening

1 🔊 8.01 **Listen to Jane and Sam discussing map apps. How do they feel about using them?**

  a They both think they are very good.

  b Neither of them like them.

  c Jane doesn't like them, but Sam does.

2 Listen again. Are the sentences true (T) or false (F)?

1 Jane travelled to Borneo alone. _____

2 Jane flew to Brunei. _____

3 They used a map app called *Find it 'n' Follow it* so that they could listen and drive. _____

4 After they turned left at the roundabout, they went into the jungle. _____

5 Jane's sister wanted to stop and go back. _____

6 They couldn't continue their journey because the road stopped. _____

7 It was early in the morning when they turned around. _____

8 They drove back to the start of their journey. _____

3a Choose the correct option a, b or c.

1 Sam wants to know why Jane has got _____ .

  a no map   b a big map   c a mobile map app

2 Sam _____ .

  a liked Jane's photos

  b wants to see Jane's photos

  c didn't know about Jane's photos

3 They used a map app called *Find it 'n' Follow it* because _____ .

  a there were no other maps

  b Jane's sister had the app

  c Jane had the app

4 At first, Sam said it was _____ to use the map app.

  a a good idea   b a bad idea   c a dangerous idea

5 The start of the journey was _____ .

  a difficult   b confusing   c easy

6 The problem was that the map app gave them _____ .

  a the wrong directions

  b too many directions

  c the directions quickly

7 The road they were driving along got _____ .

  a bigger   b smaller   c more dangerous

8 Sam _____ map apps.

  a thinks Jane should use

  b can understand why Jane doesn't like

  c wants to show Jane how to use

b Listen again and check.

Reading

1 **Read the article about travelling. Which topic isn't mentioned?**

   a types of transport

   b people who travel

   c people who never travel

   d reasons for travelling

2 **Read the article. Are the sentences true (T) or false (F)?**

   1 Everybody has travelled to another country these days. _____

   2 Nowadays, all kinds of people travel. _____

   3 About eight million people travel by car every day. _____

   4 A hundred and fifty years ago, you needed a lot of money to travel. _____

   5 In the past two centuries, there haven't been many changes in the way people travel. _____

   6 In the past, people usually lived close to their friends and families. _____

   7 In the past, it was quick and easy to travel from London to Paris. _____

   8 These days, people travel for their holidays and to see their friends and families. _____

3 **Read the article again. Choose the correct alternatives.**

   1 Long ago, people used to travel in *the same/a different* way from today.

   2 People of *all/some* ages travel these days.

   3 About eight million people are *driving/ flying* every day.

   4 When people started to travel in aeroplanes, *more/fewer* people travelled in ships.

   5 In the past, some people travelled because they *wanted/didn't want* to do business.

   6 You *had/didn't have* to be rich to travel.

   7 These days, lots of people *love/don't love* travelling.

   8 In the future, people *won't/might* travel to the moon.

4 **Match the words and phrases in bold in the text with definitions 1–5.**

   1 flying _____

   2 many _____

   3 a hundred years _____

   4 in place of _____

   5 easy to do _____

We've travelled far!

Nowadays, most people have travelled to another country. But things used to be very different. How has travel changed over the years?

Every day, people go on journeys. All around the world, you can find people at airports, train stations and on the roads. Teachers, bankers, waiters, young people and old people are now taking planes, trains and cars to get to places. About eight million people are **in the skies** each day! We think this is normal and it's obviously something which many people often do. But things were very different not so long ago, when only very rich people could travel.

The way people travelled started to change during the nineteenth **century**. Before then, people used to ride horses to get around their country. Then railways and trains were built. This made it possible for people to travel from one part of the country to another. Later, cars were invented and good roads were built. This made it faster and cheaper for ordinary people to travel around. Long-distance travel became **available** for more people. **Instead of** using ships to travel to other countries, more people started to fly in aeroplanes. Change didn't happen immediately. It happened slowly. Over **a number of** years, it became easier and easier for people to travel.

It is not only how we travel which has changed. The reasons why we travel have also changed. In the late nineteenth and early twentieth century, people travelled because they wanted to do business or because they were very rich. Most people lived near to their friends and family, so they didn't need to travel far to visit them. Most people didn't travel to another country for business or holidays. To travel from London to Paris would take six days and many different horses. This was not something most people wanted to do!

Over the past two hundred years, there have been a lot of changes in who travels, how they travel and why they travel. Now, many people love travelling. When they have a holiday, they like to travel to another country. Lots of people have friends and family all over the world. Who knows where the next one hundred years will take us? Maybe to the moon and back!

8

Writing

1 Read Helen's blog post about her holiday. Answer the questions.

1 What country is she in? ....
2 What transport is she using? ....
3 When is she leaving the South Island? ....

Hi, everyone! It's day eight of my campervan holiday around New Zealand. I've wanted to come here for ages and I'm so happy I did. It really is a dream holiday! I love travelling in the campervan because I can drive everywhere and park anywhere!

Today is my last day on the South Island and I'm in Mount Cook! It's such a beautiful place. This morning I got up early so I could watch the sun come up. The colours of the flowers and the sky are amazing! Have a look at the photos I posted on my social media account here.

Last week I went to some amazing places, too. I started my trip in Paradise Valley last Monday. The blue lakes and the mountains were incredible! Then last Wednesday, I went to Lake Tekapo and swam in the water, and last Friday I drove to Wanaka Lake. It's very pretty there. I went fishing, and cooked and ate the fish. It was so much fun! I arrived in Mount Cook the day before yesterday. I'm sad to leave this place but I'm also excited to go to the North Island.

Tomorrow, I will arrive in Rotorua, on the North Island. I'm going to park the van and ride a bike to the blue lakes. The day after tomorrow, I'm going to drive up to Lang's Beach and relax for a few days. Then next week, I'd like to visit Coromandel and walk in the beautiful mountains. I fly home the week after next!

2 Read the blog post again. Put the events in Helen's holiday in the correct order.

go fishing	....	watch the sun rise	....
relax on beach	....	visit Paradise Valley	_1_
swim in Lake Tekapo	....	visit Coromandel	....
go to the North Island	....	go to Mount Cook	....

3 Read the Focus box then underline the time expressions in the blog post.

Time expressions

Use time expressions to say when things happened or are going to happen. They can usually go at the beginning or end of a phrase or sentence.

I started college **last week**.
Next Saturday I'm going to the cinema with Jane.
Shall we watch a film **tonight**?
I'm going to Spain **the week after next**.

Some other common time expressions are: *yesterday, the day before yesterday, last Tuesday, today, this morning/afternoon/evening, tomorrow, next week/month/year, the day after tomorrow.*

4 Choose the correct alternatives.

1 *Tomorrow/ The day before yesterday*, we're going on a boat trip down the Mekong river.
2 We arrived in the South of France *the day after tomorrow/ last night*.
3 *This morning/ Tomorrow morning*, I got up early to go fishing.
4 *Today/ Last night*, I'm relaxing in the park.
5 We drove to Bondi Beach *next Friday/ last Tuesday*.
6 *Yesterday/ Next week*, we're flying to Japan.
7 *The week after next/ Last week*, we were skiing in the mountains.
8 We've organised a picnic at the lake *the day after tomorrow/ yesterday*.

Prepare

5 You're going to write a blog post about a dream holiday you are having. First, decide where you are. Then complete the travel notes with interesting places and activities.

Saturday 10th August: ....
Monday: ....
Wednesday: ....
Friday: ....
Monday: ....
Tuesday: ....
Thursday: ....
Saturday 24th: ....

Write

6 Write your latest blog post: the day is Sunday 18th August. Say what you're doing today. Then describe what you've done recently and talk about your future plans. Use some time expressions.

Vocabulary

Describing a relationship

1 **Choose the correct alternatives.**

1 Do you find it easy to *meet/make* friends with people in new situations?

2 Joe and Billy often *argue/get on* about the housework.

3 I hope we can *meet/keep* in touch after this course finishes.

4 We try to go out with all our *old/young* friends once a year.

5 I'm lucky that I *keep/get* on with all my colleagues.

6 Let's *see/meet* up next week for a coffee.

7 We'd love to *see/argue with* you all again at next year's conference.

8 My boss *keeps in touch/disagrees* with everything I suggest.

9 When I have a problem, I talk to my *near/close* friends.

2 **Complete the sentences with the words in the box.**

> argue   close   disagree   friend   get on   make
> meet   see   text   touch

1 I always _____ with my brother. He never listens to what I say!

2 Children spend too much time on their phones. They _____ each other all the time.

3 I see Ailsa every weekend – she's a really _____ friend.

4 Why do you always _____ with everything I say?

5 James is a great _____ – we _____ really well.

6 I'm so sad you're leaving. Please keep in _____ !

7 I like trying new things because it's a good way to _____ new friends.

8 I haven't seen you for months! Shall we _____ up soon?

9 I _____ my sister about once a month – we usually go shopping together.

Grammar

Present perfect with *for* and *since*

3 **Put the words in the correct order to make sentences.**

1 for a week / done / Sue / any homework / hasn't
_____

2 at / have / They / for two hours / the beach / been
_____

3 Dolly / for months / called / hasn't / me
_____

4 to university / has / lots of / Roger / since / friends / made / he went
_____

5 Jim / for five years / has / a dog / had
_____

6 sent / They / since / a birthday card / we argued / haven't / me
_____

7 in Argentina / for 15 years / lived / Ana / has
_____

8 we were / since / been / at school / We / close friends / have
_____

4 **Choose the correct alternatives.**

1 Greg and Christine have lived here *for/since* over five years.

2 There hasn't been a new company director *for/since* 2015.

3 I've known Michael *for/since* six months.

4 Jude says he hasn't been in touch with his old classmates *for/since* a long time.

5 He's been off work *for/since* Tuesday last week.

6 We haven't eaten *for/since* eight o'clock this morning.

7 I've been on holiday *for/since* 15th July.

8 I've only worked here *for/since* a month.

5 **Complete the conversation with the correct form of the verbs in brackets and *for* or *since*.**

A: Hey, Rory. How are you? I didn't know you worked here.

B: Oh Pete. Yes, I **1**_____ (work) here **2**_____ a week now.

A: Oh great! I **3**_____ (be) here **4**_____ June last year. I enjoy working here. **5**_____ you _____ (move) to the area?

B: Yes, I **6**_____ (live) in the area **7**_____ February. I love it!

A: Great! And How's your sister? Is she still working in Australia?

B: Yes, she **8**_____ (be) there **9**_____ three years now! I don't think she's going to come back!

Vocabulary

Adjectives to describe films and TV programmes

1 **Choose the correct alternatives.**

1 It's a really *long/serious* film – we were in the cinema for three and a half hours!
2 It was a really *scary/funny* film, I couldn't stop laughing!
3 I hate watching sport on TV. I think it's really *boring/long*.
4 It's a *true/popular* story about a woman who travels around the word.
5 Everyone I know has watched that film, it's really *sad/popular*.
6 I don't like watching *sad/clever* films, I want to laugh not cry!
7 It's about a dog who can speak – it's very *sad/silly*!
8 We watched a really *scary/funny* film last night. I didn't want to be alone afterwards!
9 Did you see the documentary about lions in Africa? It was really *interesting/true*.

2 **Complete the sentences with the words in the box.**

boring   clever   exciting   long   sad   scary
serious   silly   true

1 I watched a programme about the _____ story of a man who found £100,000 on the street!
2 It's a really _____ programme because it makes you think.
3 It was a good film, but it was too _____. I fell asleep watching it!
4 I didn't like that film – it was too _____. I prefer funny films.
5 I love that programme! It's very _____, but it makes me laugh!
6 The film was really _____ – it made me cry!
7 There are many _____ things to do and see at the festival.
8 It was a really _____ film. I stopped watching it after half an hour!
9 I think crime dramas are _____, so I never watch them alone. I get frightened easily!

Grammar

Present perfect with *already*, *just* and *yet*

3 **Complete the sentences with the correct form of the verbs in brackets.**

1 Jill and Alison _____ (not go) on holiday yet this year.
2 She _____ already _____ (forget) everything she learnt on the training course.
3 I _____ just _____ (see) my best friend in the library.
4 The children _____ just _____ (eat) their dinner.
5 I _____ (not tell) anybody your news yet.
6 Richi _____ just _____ (buy) a new house close to the river.
7 I _____ already _____ (finish) painting the kitchen.
8 The doctor _____ (not give) me any new exercises to do yet.

4 **Put the words in the correct order to make sentences.**

1 been / new café / Have / to the / yet / you?
_____
2 the books / already / you / have / I / given / you wanted
_____
3 Ben's / haven't / yet / I / new girlfriend / met
_____
4 to go / have / left / They / to the station / just
_____
5 baked / Dotty / already / the cake / has / for the party
_____
6 a new book / just / Simon / has / writing / finished
_____

5 **Complete the sentences with *just, yet* or *already*.**

1 Wait a minute! I've _____ got here!
2 Peter hasn't seen all the pictures from the party _____ .
3 I'm going to have a shower. I've _____ run all the way home.
4 Can we do something else? I've _____ been to the cinema twice this week.
5 Paul's plane landed hours ago, but he's not here _____ .
6 They've _____ started the race, so you haven't missed anything.
7 Have you told your brother about your visit _____ ?
8 Don't feed the cat because I've _____ fed it today.
9 I'm not telling you again. I've _____ told you twice!

9c

Vocabulary

Education

1 **Complete the sentences with the words in the box.**

at (x5) do (x2) find (x3) for in pass take

1 Jenny is studying _____ her diploma in Spanish.
2 I used to be terrible _____ working with computers.
3 I can't go out tonight. I have to _____ an exam tomorrow.
4 What were you good _____ when you were at school?
5 I'm not happy when I _____ badly at something.
6 You will get better _____ tennis if you practise.
7 I _____ cooking easy, even when I'm cooking for a lot of people.
8 Simon really wants to _____ well in his new job.
9 I _____ these computers difficult to use.
10 We all worked hard _____ getting the work finished on time.
11 I'm good at dancing but bad _____ singing.
12 Steph is interested _____ playing golf.
13 Did you _____ the film boring?
14 You're so clever that I'm sure you'll _____ the exam.

2 **Match the sentence halves.**

1 I hope my sister does _____
2 John is able to pass _____
3 Phoebe said she's interested _____
4 Cleaning is something I find _____
5 I need some help because I'm terrible _____
6 Tom thought he'd do _____

a really boring!
b exams without studying a lot.
c badly in the match, but he won!
d in travelling to Mexico.
e at maths.
f well in her first French exam today.

3 **Correct the mistake in each sentence.**

1 I have working in a café difficult. I can't concentrate.

2 She's busy studying in her economics exams at university.

3 I want to get well in the fun run, so I run every day.

4 I got my English exam yesterday. I think I passed.

5 I want to be good in photography and then I can start my own photography business.

6 Over the years, I've got better on painting pictures.

Grammar

could/couldn't

4 **Choose the correct option a, b or c.**

1 When I first moved to this town, I couldn't _____ my way around.
   a to find   b found   c find
2 I couldn't _____ the story in that film. Could you?
   a understood   b to understand   c understand
3 Tim couldn't _____ when he first joined the band.
   a sung   b sing   c to sing
4 I couldn't _____ any French when I moved to France last year.
   a speak   b to speak   c spoke
5 When Simon was eight, he could _____ all the capital cities in the world.
   a remembered   b remember   c to remember
6 Jo couldn't _____ a horse when she was young, but she's expert now.
   a ride   b to ride   c rode

5 **Complete the sentences with could/couldn't and the verbs in the box.**

decide make remember run stay awake travel understand write

1 My parents were very happy that I _____ my breakfast when I was only ten years old.
2 Chris _____ until he was nearly eight, but now he's a journalist.
3 I _____ why studying was important when I was at school, and I didn't enjoy it.
4 Maria says she _____ anyone's name, but then she learnt a way to help her.
5 Gordon _____ faster than all his classmates because he had such long legs.
6 I _____ what to wear for the party, but then my sister helped me.
7 Aeroplanes _____ long distances when they first started flying.
8 I _____ for the whole opera because it was too long.

Functional language

Ask for information politely

1 Choose the correct alternatives.

1 **A:** Could you tell me the where the bread is?
   B: Yes, *of / if* course. It's at the back of the store.

2 **A:** Do you *think / know* if I can use my credit card in that shop?
   B: Yes, I think you can.

3 **A:** Do you know what the time is?
   B: I'm sorry, *I'm not / I don't*.

4 **A:** *Do / Could* you tell me where the nearest bank is?
   B: Yes, of course. Take a left and go straight on.

5 **A:** Do you know if I can take the bus with this ticket?
   B: *I'm not / I don't* sure. You'll have to ask the driver.

6 **A:** Excuse me. *Could / Do* you tell me if the ticket is cheaper for students?
   B: Sure. Students get ten percent off the entrance price.

7 **A:** Do you *tell me / know* where I can buy a train ticket?
   B: Sure. You can buy a ticket over there.

8 **A:** Could you tell me the wifi code?
   B: I'm *afraid / sure* I can't help you with that. I don't know it.

2 Cross out one extra word in sentences 1–8.

A: Hi there. Thanks for stopping. ¹Do you know ~~how~~ the way to Hotel Marazion?

B: ²Yes, of a course, get in.

A: Thanks. ³Could you tell me if how much this journey will cost?

B: ⁴I'm afraid no I can't. It depends on the traffic.

A: Oh … OK. ⁵Do you know how much long it might take to get there?

B: ⁶I'm not of sure. It shouldn't take more than 30 minutes.

A: And ⁷do you know what if there is a supermarket near the hotel?

B: ⁸I'm sorry, I am don't. But you can ask at the hotel when you arrive.

3 Rewrite the questions so they are more polite.

1 Where is the ticket office?
   Do ____*you know where the ticket office*____ is?

2 How much is a return ticket?
   Could _____ costs?

3 Is there a toilet on the train?
   Do _____ train?

4 What time does the next train leave?
   Could _____ leaves?

5 Is there a bank near here?
   Do _____ here?

6 How long does the journey take?
   Do _____ takes?

Listening

1 ◁)) 9.01 Listen to the first part of a radio interview. Choose the correct alternatives.

1 Janet *is / isn't* paid to watch films.

2 Janet *gives companies advice / sells companies films*.

3 Live TV has become *more / less* popular.

2 ◁)) 9.02 Listen to the second part of the interview. Are the sentences true (T) or false (F)?

1 Janet watches TV programmes on TV channels. ____

2 Thirty percent of adults under 40 don't watch any traditional TV. ____

3 Young people don't like TV programmes. ____

4 Young people use apps to watch TV programmes. ____

5 Lots of young people still go to the cinema. ____

6 You can watch online TV when you want. ____

7 Companies don't want to pay for adverts on TV anymore. ____

8 TV companies aren't worried. ____

3 Listen to the second part again. Choose the correct option, a or b.

1 Older people's TV habits …
   a have changed.   **b** haven't changed.

2 Young people don't like watching …
   a TV programmes.   **b** live TV.

3 Many young people prefer to watch films …
   a at home.   **b** at the cinema.

4 Young people stopped renting DVDs because …
   a it took too much time.
   b they didn't want to see them.

5 If young people don't watch live TV …
   a they don't see adverts.
   b they don't pay for adverts.

6 Jane thinks companies should …
   a buy apps.   **b** buy advertisements in apps.

Reading

1 Read the text and choose the best title a, b or c.

a Seven kinds of friend

b Six good friends and one bad friend

c What kind of friend are you?

2 Read the text again. Which paragraph 1–7 describes ...

a a friend who can help you learn about other cultures? ....

b a friend who is happy to help with your future? ....

c a friend who likes very different things from you? ....

d a friend who won't try to change you? ....

e a friend who other people always like? ....

f a friend you see a lot of during the week? ....

g a friend who won't lie to you? ....

3 Read the text again. Are the sentences true (T) or false (F)?

1 We don't learn much from someone with a lot of life experience. ....

2 We usually get on well with people who like the same things as us. ....

3 We can tell a true friend things we don't want other people to know. ....

4 Life is difficult at work when we share problems with our friends there. ....

5 Friends from other cultures don't teach us new things. ....

6 Friends sometimes lie because we might not like the truth. ....

7 Popular people aren't usually sure of themselves. ....

4 Find words 1–6 in the text and match them with definitions a–f below.

1 advice (paragraph 1) ....

2 patient (paragraph 1) ....

3 respect (paragraph 1/2) ....

4 get on (paragraph 2) ....

5 honest (paragraph 6) ....

6 popular (paragraph 7) ....

a ideas about things to do or say

b tells the truth

c to have a good relationship with someone

d doesn't get angry easily

e liked by a lot of people

f to have good thoughts about someone

1

This friend has a lot of life experience and can give you good advice. They teach you a lot and help you become a better person. This person is often older than you, and they have done many things in their life, so you respect them. They are patient with you and want to guide you.

2

Usually, you spend time with friends who are similar to you. This is why you get on so well. But not this friend! No, this friend is totally different from you. People ask, 'Why are you two friends?' This friend has very different opinions and they like different kinds of films and music. This makes you respect them because they can help you think differently, too.

3

Everyone needs a friend like this. Someone who will always agree with you. You can tell them all your secrets because you know you can trust them. This friend loves you for who you are. They don't let other people say bad things about you, and they understand when you make mistakes. Some people say this is a true friend!

4

We spend a lot of our lives at work and this friend makes work fun. You can complain about your boss with them or you can talk about how much work you have got. They make your work life easier because they share the same problems as you. You might not spend a lot of time with them outside of your work, but they are an important part of your life.

5

This kind of friend is great because they are different. They have grown up in another culture and they have different life experiences. This friend can teach you a lot about other people and their traditions and opinions. They can really change you and bring new experiences into your life.

6

If everyone told the truth all the time, we might not like it! For this reason, friends sometimes lie. The lies are often about small things and people sometimes lie to be kind. Lying might stop arguments, but it can create a new problem. What if we need someone to tell us the truth? You can always ask your honest friend for their real opinion. They will tell you the truth, even if you don't like it!

7

This friend doesn't worry about meeting new people. They know they are popular and look good. They always look happy and they are very confident. Other people always say, 'He's so great!' or 'She's so funny!' You take this friend to parties because they will make everything easier and more fun.

9

Writing

1 Read the two job applications. Complete them with the correct job, a or b.
a dental assistant
b weekend theatre lighting assistant

---

1 Dear Sir or Madam,

I am writing to apply for the position of _____ .
Please find my CV attached.

I am at university, studying theatre management. Last summer, I worked at my local theatre for eight weeks. During this time, I learnt a lot about lighting technology, which I think will be useful in the role you are offering.

I am available for an interview in the evenings or at the weekends. If you would like any more information, please contact me at this email address or by phone. I look forward to hearing from you.

Your faithfully,

Jenny O'Reilly

---

2 Dear Sir or Madam,

I am writing to apply for the position of _____ , as advertised in *Dental Today Weekly*. I have attached a copy of my CV.

This year, I have worked in a dental clinic, helping the dentists with all areas of patient care. I am also studying part-time for my dental nurse qualification. I believe my studies and experience will be very useful in the role you have advertised.

I am available for an interview during office hours. If you would like any more information, please contact me by phone. I look forward to hearing from you.

Yours faithfully,

Marion Osley

---

2 Read the job applications again and answer the questions. Write Jenny (J), Marion (M) or both (J/M).
1 Who saw the job advertisement in the media? _____
2 Who is studying full-time? _____
3 Who has more work experience? _____
4 Who is available for interview during the day? _____
5 Who has experience that is useful for the job? _____
6 Who can be contacted by telephone only? _____

3 Read the Focus box. Which of the formal phrases in the box are in the emails in Exercise 1.

Formal phrases

It's important to use formal phrases when writing an application for a job because they make it sound polite and professional. They can also help you with the structure of the letter or email. Some formal phrases which are useful in a letter or email application are:
Dear Sir or Madam
I am writing to apply for the position of …
Please find attached …
During this time …
I am available for an interview at any time.
I look forward to hearing from you.
Yours faithfully,

4 Put the words in the correct order to make sentences.
1 to apply / I / school counsellor / of / am / the position / writing / for
2 attached / find / my CV / Please
3 the latest research / During / I learnt / this / about / time
4 to hearing / look / from you / forward / I
5 I / interview / am / available / any / at / for / time / an

5 Replace the informal phrases with formal phrases in the Focus box.

¹Hi,
²I want the job of shop assistant at the Bella Boutique in Coventry. ³I'm sending my CV with this email.
I have worked in shops for many years and ⁴while I was there I learnt about sales and customer service.
⁵I'm free to talk to you any time.
⁶I hope you reply soon.
⁷Goodbye
Gerry Lake

Prepare

6a You're going to write a job application. Choose one of the jobs in the box to apply for.

computer programmer   shop assistant   tour guide
TV presenter   waiter

b Answer these questions and make notes.
• What is your previous experience?
• What qualifications do you have/are you studying for?
• Why would you be good for the job?
• When are you available?

Write

7 Write your job application. Use your notes in Exercise 6 and the formal phrases in the Focus box to help you.

10A

Vocabulary

Money

1 Complete the missing words.

1 **A:** Help! I spend too much money each week. How can
I s_____ money?

   B: You should be more careful. Try not to buy things
that c_____ a lot.

   A: Maybe I should give up smoking. I w_____ a lot
of money on cigarettes.

2 **A:** You should buy those shoes. They're great!

   B: Are you serious? I don't e_____ enough money
to buy them!

3 **A:** Can you l_____ me £2?

   B: What for?

   A: I have to pay for this pen with c_____, but I only
have my card.

4 **A:** Excuse me. How much is this jacket?

   B: It's £95, sir.

   A: Can I p_____ f_____ it by c_____ card?

5 **A:** I haven't got any money left! Could I b_____
£10?

   B: Why haven't you got any money?

   A: I had to s_____ it all on a present for my
girlfriend!

2 Match the sentence halves.

1 Oh no, I've forgotten my purse! Can I borrow ____

2 Do you like my new jacket? It cost ____

3 I want to get a new job so I can earn ____

4 I lent my friend Enzo ____

5 I went shopping yesterday and spent ____

6 The meal was terrible. I wasted ____

7 I always pay for ____

8 I try to save ____

a more money than I do now.

b things by credit card. I never have any cash!

c lots of money on new clothes!

d £5 please? I promise I'll pay you back tomorrow!

e money every month, but I usually spend it all!

f all my money on it. I won't go there again.

g £10 last week because he didn't have any cash.

h a lot of money!

Grammar

First conditional

3 Choose the correct alternatives.

1 If you *like*/*'ll like* rock music, you *love*/*'ll love* this
new band!

2 I *call*/*'ll call* you later if I *have*/*'ll have* time.

3 If she *passes*/*'ll pass* her exam, she *goes*/*'ll go* to
university.

4 You *won't*/*don't remember* the vocabulary if you
won't/*don't* do your homework.

5 If you *are*/*'ll be* going out later, you *need*/*'ll need*
a jacket.

6 I *have*/*'ll have* a picnic if the weather *is*/*'ll be* nice.

7 You *waste*/*'ll waste* money if you *buy*/*'ll buy* things you
don't need.

8 If you *don't*/*won't* save money now, you *don't*/*won't* be
able to go on holiday.

**4 Write sentences using the prompts. Use the first
conditional.**

1 you / only buy what you need / you / save money
If *you only buy what you need, you'll save money* .

2 you / should not buy expensive things /
want to save money
You _____ .

3 you / use special offers from newspapers and magazines /
you / spend less
If _____ .

4 you / find more discounts / shop in the evening
You _____ .

5 you / use a shopping app / it / help save you money
If _____ .

6 can find better prices / you / visit more than one
supermarket
You _____ .

5 Complete the sentences with the words in the box.

can   don't   if   shouldn't   want   will   won't   you

1 If you have an old phone, you _____ sell it on online.

2 If you _____ book now, the plane ticket will be
more expensive.

3 If you _____ to save money in a restaurant, you can
share a dessert.

4 You should get there on time _____ you leave now.

5 You won't lose weight if _____ don't do regular
exercise.

6 If you walk to work, you _____ save money.

7 You _____ have any money when you're older if
you don't save now.

8 You _____ use a credit card if you don't have any
money.

10B

Grammar

Present and past passive

1 Choose the correct alternatives.

1 Coffee *discovered/was discovered* in Ethopia, 800 years ago.
2 In the past, coffee *called/was called* 'Qahwah'.
3 Before people drank coffee, they *ate/was eaten* it.
4 Coffee *grows/is grown* well in warm countries.
5 40% of the world's coffee *made/is made* in Brazil.
6 80% of American adults *drink/are drunk* coffee.
7 42 coffee beans *use/are used* to make one espresso.
8 British people *spend/is spent* more than £700 million on coffee every year.

2 Complete the sentences with the correct active or passive form of the verbs in brackets.

1 The washing machine _____ (invent) in 1906.
2 600 million lightbulbs _____ (use) in the UK every day.
3 The first iPod _____ (sell) in 2001.
4 99% of American homes _____ (have) at least one TV.
5 200 billion emails _____ (send) around the world every day.
6 The first aeroplane _____ (fly) in 1903.
7 8 million fridges _____ (buy) in the US every year.
8 Alexander Bell _____ (make) the first phone call in 1876.

3 Rewrite the sentences using the passive.

1 One person didn't invent virtual reality.
Virtual reality *wasn't invented by one person* .
2 Many people worked on the idea of virtual reality.
The idea of virtual reality _____ .
3 Jaron Lanier chose the name *virtual reality* in 1987.
The name *virtual reality* _____ .
4 In the beginning, people used virtual reality for computer games.
In the beginning, _____ .
5 These days, both kids and adults enjoy virtual reality games.
Virtual reality games _____ .
6 The US army uses virtual reality.
Virtual reality _____ .
7 Doctors help people using virtual reality.
People _____ .
8 Last year, people spent more than $15 billion dollars on virtual reality.
More _____ .

Vocabulary

Time expressions

4 Choose the correct alternatives.

1 It's strange to think we didn't have mobile phones 20 years *ago/before*.
2 People eat more sugar *these/those* days than in the past.
3 *For a long time/Ago*, people believed the world was flat.
4 I didn't have a mobile phone *for a long time/until* 2007.
5 James fell asleep *during/for* the meeting this morning!
6 *Each/These* day, they walk to the river to collect water.
7 I'm really interested in 19th-*century/time* history.
8 I used to ride a bike to work, but *until/nowadays* I get the bus.
9 *During/For a long time* the summer, I worked in a restaurant.
10 I posted your birthday card *until three days/three days ago*.

5 Put the words in brackets in the correct place in the sentences.

during
1 I hate it when people talk/the film. (during)
2 I won't finish work six thirty this evening! (until)
3 We don't see each other much days. (these)
4 The first film was made in the late 19th. (century)
5 A few years, I went to China for the first time. (ago)
6 You're late! I've been waiting 45 minutes! (for)
7 I love you more day. (each)
8 Almost everyone has a mobile phone. (nowadays)

Grammar

Review of tenses

1 Complete the text with the past simple or past continuous form of the verbs in brackets.

When I was young, my dad **1**_____ (always have) lots of different hobbies. He **2**_____ (be) always busy doing something new. When he **3**_____ (not work), he **4**_____ (spend) his free time on his hobbies. One of his hobbies was his car. He **5**_____ (love) that car. I used to watch him when he **6**_____ (work) on it. One day, he **7**_____ (do) something to the car and he looked up and asked me, 'Why don't you get a hobby, son?' I realised I **8**_____ (have) no idea which hobby I wanted to do!

2 Complete the text with the present simple, present continuous or present perfect form of the verbs in brackets.

A hobby **1**_____ (be) a good way to relax, but I **2**_____ never _____ (have) a special interest. After trying lots of different activities, I **3**_____ finally _____ (find) my perfect hobby! So I **4**_____ (want) to share some advice with you. If you **5**_____ (not find) a hobby you enjoy yet, or if you **6**_____ (look) for one right now, this is what to do.

You **7**_____ (need) to think about your personality and the things you **8**_____ (enjoy) doing all your life. Ask yourself: what **9**_____ I _____ (look for)?

3 Choose the correct alternatives.

Six steps to finding the perfect hobby

1 Understand that finding your hobby **1***won't be/ isn't being* easy. It **2***is taking/will take* some time.

2 Think about how much free time you will have. **3***Are you going to have/Are you having* some free time soon or do you have lots of social arrangements? If you **4***will do/are doing* a lot in the next few weeks, maybe wait until you have some free time.

3 Think about money. You need to predict how much money you **5***will spend/are spending* on the hobby.

4 Consider if you **6***will enjoy/are enjoying* working alone or with other people.

5 Think about what you are good at. Don't choose something that you **7***won't be/aren't being* good at.

6 Remember that if you **8***are going to do/will do* the hobby, it needs to be exciting.

If you follow this advice, I'm sure you will find the right hobby for you!

4 Write sentences using the prompts. Use the correct verb forms.

1 My friends / come to / my house / tonight
_____

2 I think / it / rain / tomorrow
_____

3 I / play volleyball / when / I / fall over
_____

4 On Fridays / I usually / eat / in a restaurant
_____

5 The baby / sleep / now
_____

6 Next year / I / change / jobs
_____

7 I / go to the shops / yesterday
_____

8 I / live here / all my life
_____

Vocabulary

Hobbies and interests

5 Complete each sentence with one word.

1 I really enjoy being part _____ a team. What do you suggest?

2 I don't want a 'serious' hobby. Can you suggest something I can do for _____?

3 Where can I learn _____ finding the right hobby?

4 I'd like to try something _____, so I'm going to learn to play the piano.

5 Where can I _____ out about new events in my area?

6 I start hobbies but then give them _____ easily.

7 I think I'm going to _____ the new art club in town.

8 I love spending _____ reading, it's really relaxing.

6 Complete the sentences with the correct form of the verbs in the box.

be   do   give   join   learn   make   spend   ~~try~~

1 John is excited when he ___*tries*___ something new.

2 I've never _____ up anything in my life. I don't quit.

3 I started _____ Judo a few weeks ago, just for fun.

4 If you _____ a club, you'll meet people who enjoy the same hobby.

5 Before I started kite surfing, I _____ sure it was safe to do!

6 We play together twice a week. It's nice to _____ part of a team.

7 I love my new painting class! I'm _____ so much about art.

8 I want to _____ more time playing football, so I'm going to join the football club.

10D

Functional language

Ask for clarification

1 Choose the correct alternatives.

1 **A:** When you arrive, call me.
   B: OK, *get*/*got* it! I should be there around nine o'clock.

2 **A:** Follow the road, turn left and then turn right. OK?
   B: *Can*/*Do* you say that again, please?

3 **A:** We're thinking of going to a 'Bring and Buy' sale in Camden tomorrow.
   B: Hmmm. *What's*/*How's* a 'Bring and Buy' sale?

4 **A:** Sally's in a funny mood today.
   B: Really? I'm not sure what you *are meaning*/*mean*.

5 **A:** We can't get the 7.40 p.m. train because we don't arrive until 8.15 p.m.
   B: Oh, I *saw*/*see*. Is there a bus we could get?

6 **A:** I don't think this plan is going to work.
   B: What do you *say*/*mean* exactly?

7 **A:** I've decided to leave my job and travel around the world.
   B: *I don't*/*I'm not* understand. Did you say you're going to leave your job?

2 Complete each conversation with the phrases in the boxes.

I'm not sure what you mean.   I see.   What's a sleeper?
What was that last part again?

A: So, you've got two options. You can take the sleeper or the Eurotrain and then local trains.
B: ¹ _____
A: Well, a sleeper is a night train with beds to sleep in. It can take you straight to where you want to go. I'm sure you don't want to chop and change.
B: ² _____
A: Chop and change? Get off one train and get on another train.
B: ³ _____
A: If you take the Eurotrain, you will need to take two or three more local trains to get to the town you want to go to. If you take the sleeper, you will go straight there.
B: ⁴ _____

Can you say that again?   I still don't understand.   Oh, got it!
What do you mean exactly?

A: Put the blue files on the left, with the red files and the green files. Oh, and don't forget to note down what, where and when.
B: ⁵ _____
A: You have to write down the name of each file, where you put it on the shelves, and the dates of the information in the file.
B: ⁶ _____
A: Sure. Write down the name of each file. Write down where you put the file on the shelves. Then write down the dates of the information in each file.
B: ⁷ _____
A: What don't you understand? OK. Let's start with the names of the files. Write these down.
B: ⁸ _____
A: Great!

10

Listening

1 🔊 10.01 Listen to a radio programme. What's it about?
   a Listening to lots of problems
   b Finding an answer to one person's problem
   c Talking about local problems

2 Listen again. Are the sentences true (T) or false (F)?

1 The presenter thinks the dilemma is very common. _____
2 Marsha wants to use some money for her house. _____
3 Marsha doesn't know who to give the rest of the money to. _____
4 There aren't many people in Marsha's family. _____
5 Marsha wants her family to have lots of money. _____
6 The emails suggest giving money to charities. _____
7 Marsha thinks the second caller's idea is bad. _____
8 The presenter feels the problem is solved. _____

3a Choose the correct option a, b or c.

1 Marsha has _____ a lot of money.
   a saved   b won   c found
2 Marsha's family have _____ ideas.
   a no   b a few   c lots of
3 The first caller thinks the solution is _____ .
   a simple   b complicated   c difficult
4 Marsha is worried her family would become too _____ money.
   a sad with   b bored with   c interested in
5 The second caller thinks Marsha should help _____ charities.
   a animal   b local   c big
6 Marsha doesn't want to help _____ .
   a birds   b her local area   c charities
7 Marsha has _____ in her local area all her life.
   a worked   b lived   c had fun
8 The presenter _____ to know what Marsha will do.
   a doesn't want   b wants   c doesn't care

b Listen again and check.

Buried treasure

Reading

1 Read the article and choose the best summary, a or b.

a It's always a good idea to throw away your old things.

b Keep your old things because they might be worth money.

2 Read the article again. Put the facts in the correct order 1–5.

a Shivon started looking for things in her local area. ....

b Shivon works in different countries. ....

c Shivon found an important painting. ....

d She found valuable things, including a handbag. ....

e Shivon studied at university. ....

3 Choose the correct alternatives.

1 The article says that *all/some* people throw things away.

2 Shivon believes you *can/can't* find interesting things in your home.

3 When Shivon was *an adult/a child,* she started to enjoy finding things.

4 Shivon had *a boring/an exciting* time when she stayed at her grandparents' farm.

5 Shivon's family *didn't know/knew* that the painting was hidden at the farm.

6 Money is *very/not very* important to Shivon.

7 After university, Shivon started working *all over the world/in her home town.*

8 The article says you *should/shouldn't* talk with Shivon before you throw away your things.

4 Match the words in bold in the text with definitions 1–6.

1 worth a lot of money ....

2 difficult to see or find ....

3 very big ....

4 something that no one thinks about anymore ....

5 rooms at the top of a house ....

6 have something because you bought it ....

What do we do with things we don't use anymore? Some people throw things away. Other people put things at the back of the cupboard and forget about them. The things could be presents they didn't want, old toys, items from their family, old clothes – anything! These things are put away and we forget about them.

Shivon O'Neill believes that you can find many interesting things in people's homes. Here's her story. When Shivon was a child, she used to spend her summer holidays at her grandparents' farm in the Wicklow Hills in Ireland.

'My grandma and grandad had a **huge** farm. I haven't got any brothers or sisters, so I spent my time at the farm playing and looking around. My family has **owned** the farm for more than 100 years. A lot of people have lived there and have put away things that they didn't want. I found **forgotten** old clothes, photos and books in different places around the old buildings. I had a wonderful time!' Shivon told us.

In one of the buildings at the farm, Shivon found a painting by a famous Irish painter. The painting was **hidden** for 60 years and no one knew! The forgotten painting was sold for a lot of money.

'Yes, of course my family was happy about getting a lot of money for the painting,' Shivon says. 'But the money wasn't so important to me. I am happy that a beautiful painting is now in someone's home and people are looking at it every day!'

At university, Shivon studied art history and woodwork. After she finished her degree, she went home to Limerick in Ireland.

'I started helping my family and neighbours. I looked in their **attics**, their garages and in all the places people use to put things away so that they can't see them every day. Some amazing things were hidden away!'

Over the next few months, Shivon found lots of **valuable** toys, paintings, clothes and many other things. She even found a handbag that used to belong to Jackie Kennedy. The things were sold for around 1.5 million euros.

These days, Shivon works all over the world finding things which are hidden in people's homes. People often have no idea that such expensive things are hidden in their homes. So, next time you are thinking about throwing away the things you aren't using anymore, maybe you should get in touch with Shivon!

Writing

1 Read the blog. Why has the writer written a wish list?

My birthday present wish list

My birthday is only six weeks away. It's a special and important birthday because I'm going to be 30 years old. My family and friends say that they would like to give me presents that I really want. So, I've written a birthday present wish list, to help them! My wish list gives a description of each present. I want to make sure that my family and friends buy me the right presents!

1 The watch

I have a very clear idea about the watch I want. It's got <u>brown</u>, <u>leather</u> straps and a <u>small</u>, <u>square</u>, <u>gold</u> watch face. The watch face has got <u>old</u>, <u>black</u> Roman numbers. It's simple and beautiful.

2 The gym bag

I go to the gym twice a week. I have always got lots of things in my bag because I go to work after the gym. I saw a <u>round</u>, <u>yellow</u> gym bag on the internet. It's got <u>wide</u>, <u>cotton</u> straps. I love it!

3 The sunglasses

It's nearly summer and I love sunglasses! I've got two pairs already, but they are <u>old</u>, <u>black</u>, <u>plastic</u> sunglasses. I think I should get a <u>new</u> pair. I saw a <u>big</u>, <u>green</u> pair at LaMode in the shopping mall. I look great in these <u>green</u>, <u>metal</u> sunglasses!

4 The trainers

The last thing on my birthday wish list is a new pair of shoes. I've seen a great pair of <u>white</u>, <u>leather</u> trainers. The black ones are cheaper, but I don't like them.

What's on your wish list?

2 Read the article again and answer the questions.

1 When is the writer's birthday?

2 Does she know what kind of watch she wants?

3 Why does she have a lot of things in her gym bag?

4 Why does she need a new pair of sunglasses?

5 What colour trainers does she want?

3 Read the Focus box. Then complete the table with the underlined adjectives in the article in Exercise 1.

Order of adjectives

To describe something using more than one adjective, use this order: size, age, shape, colour, material + object.

However, try not to use more than two or three adjectives at a time. To do this you should choose the adjectives that best describe the object.

I would like a round, yellow gym bag.

… they are old, black, plastic sunglasses.

Use a comma between each adjective.

size	
age	
shape	
colour	brown
material	

4 Put the words in the correct order to make sentences.

1 lost / big / I've / earrings / my / silver

2 old / trousers / I / cotton / found / blue / a pair of

3 round / cake / My mum / made a / big / pink

4 pencil case / red / in the classroom / I left my / plastic / new

5 big / sofa / I bought a / leather / square

6 denim / got my / shorts / blue / Have you / old?

Prepare

5a Think about four presents you would like for your next birthday.

b Describe each present using two or three adjectives. Put the adjectives in the correct order.

1

2

3

4

Write

6 Write your birthday wish list. Use your notes in Exercise 5 and the Focus box to help you.

AUDIO SCRIPTS

Recording 1

P = Presenter   J = Jack

P: So, we all think saying hello and goodbye is easy ... a simple 'hi' or 'bye' – and job done! In many cases this is true, but is it the whole story? Well, I'd like to introduce Jack Tunnel, who is an English language expert. Jack, we would like you to teach us a little bit about greetings in different countries.

J: 'Hello there!' or 'Hey! What's up?' Yes, you're right. There are so many ways to say hello and goodbye in different English-speaking countries. Let me share a few examples with you.

P: OK, great! Um, can you tell us how people in Australia say hello and goodbye?

J: Yes, I can. Australia has some interesting greetings. To say hello, you can say 'G'day' or 'How ya going?', and to say goodbye, it's 'Cheerio' or 'Toodle-oo'! That's quite different from a normal 'hi' and 'bye', don't you think?

P: Wow! Yes, that is different. What greetings from other English-speaking countries can you tell us about?

J: Well, how about the US? In the US, to say hello, people might say 'Hey! What's up?' or 'What's happening?'. To say goodbye, they might say 'Take it easy' or 'Catch ya later'. Now, in Ireland, it's also very different. 'What's the story?' and 'How's it going there?' is how some people like to say hello. Also, people in Ireland often don't say goodbye to one another. They just leave!

P: What? They leave with no goodbye! That's so interesting – I didn't know that.

J: I have one more example to share. In Scotland, to say hello you can say 'All right' or 'How you going?', and to say goodbye you can say 'See you after' or 'Ta ta for now'. I think these Scottish greetings are my favourite. They sound so friendly!

P: Well, there you have it, listeners! Many thanks, Jack, for coming on to our programme to teach us a few new ways to say hello and goodbye. So, from me, I'll now say cheerio, catch ya later and ta ta for now! Next up, with the news ...

Recording 1

A People say that food in England is bad, but I disagree. We have a lot of fantastic dishes ... and this is one of them. It's a hot pie that has meat and vegetables inside, usually potatoes, onions and carrots. It's called a beef pasty. You can hold a pasty in your hand and eat it. It's a complete meal! People first ate pasties around 400 years ago, and they are still popular today. Many people like to eat them with tomato ketchup. They are really tasty to eat, especially on a cold day. You can buy them in supermarkets and in bakeries, and some pubs serve them.

B Another English dish that I really like is called bubble and squeak. My mum made it for me when I was a child. My grandmother showed Mum how to make it. It's made with food left from last night's dinner. It's usually cabbage and potato. You mix this with meat, usually beef, and then cook it all together. It's called bubble and squeak because it makes a strange sound when you cook it. It doesn't look nice, but it tastes great! People first started eating bubble and squeak in England around 300 years ago. It's still popular today, but you can't find it in shops or restaurants, you have to make it at home.

C My last example of English food is different because it's sweet! It's a round cake that comes from a town called Eccles in Manchester. People think that the first Eccles cake was made there around 300 years ago. The cake is covered in sugar and it's delicious. Inside the cake there are lots of different types of fruit, usually bits of orange, lemon and currants. Currants are small dried grapes. Eccles cakes aren't very healthy, because they're made with a lot of butter. The best place to try an Eccles cake is in a bakery, where they are fresh and made by hand. But be careful. One Eccles cake is never enough!

Recording 1

J = Jen   A = Angus

J: Hi, Angus. How have you been?

A: Great, thanks.

J: You've been on holiday recently, right?

A: Yes, I have. I'm really sad it's finished. It was too short.

J: Yeah, I know what you mean! It's hard to go back to work after a long holiday. Did you go somewhere nice?

A: Yes, I did. I took the train up to Fort William and spent two weeks skiing on Ben Nevis!

J: Skiing? Really?! I loved going skiing when I was younger! My mum and dad took us all the time when we were kids ... But they're too old now and my friends prefer hot weather.

A: Yeah, my friends like summer weather, too. That's why I went alone!

J: Wait. You were on your own?

A: Yeah – I like being alone. I can practise my skiing and it's so beautiful on the mountain that you don't really need to speak to other people.

J: Oh no! I'd go crazy. I need to talk to people!

A: Well, of course you can talk to people. There are lots of people at the ski centre. Everyone is very friendly.

J: Huh. Was it expensive?

A: Not really. A day pass costs £20 and you can find cheap places to stay, too. I stayed in a little wooden cabin. It even had an outdoor Jacuzzi!

J: Nice! Maybe my friends *would* like a winter holiday!

A: I highly recommend it. I go every year. There is a lot to do and there are lots of good restaurants to eat in. But the best part is the amazing views! I took some great photos there!

J: Is it difficult to get to?

A: No, it's easier than you think. About four and a half hours' train journey from Edinburgh.

J: Wow. I think I might go skiing next holiday!

J = Jess   D = Danny   P = Pauline

J: Thanks for coming, everyone! We're here to organise a full-day celebration next month.

D: The whole day! That's a lot. Why can't we just have a celebration in the evening?

P: I agree with Jess. It's the 50th birthday of our company, so we should have a really good celebration.

J: Thank you, Pauline. That's right. We're celebrating 50 years.

D: OK, good point. So, what would you like us to do?

J: Well, we have to find a big venue so that everyone in the company can come. We also have to plan some activities for people to do at the party.

D: What sorts of activities will everyone like? It's not going to be easy!

J: I think we should plan some sports activities, like cricket or baseball.

D: Great idea!

P: I hate sport, especially cricket, and not everyone will be able to play it. How about something everyone can do, like a murder mystery day? It'll be fun!

J: Hmm ... I suppose it's true that not everyone likes sport. I would like a celebration everyone enjoys because this is a day to say 'thank you' to everyone in the company. How does a murder mystery day work?

D: I went to a murder mystery day last year. Actors do a murder mystery play and the people at the party have to watch and decide who the murderer is. We are the detectives.

P: That's right! We watch, listen and talk about what happened. Then we guess the murderer. It's a lot more fun than cricket!

J: That's a good idea. Let's have a murder mystery day, then. So, who's going to do what?

P: I'll look for a venue.

D: And I'll book the actors!

J: Sounds good! Let's meet next week to decide our plans for the evening. We need to plan the food and the music, too.

J = Jennifer   C = Charlie   V = Vicky

J: Hi, Charlie, come in.

C: Thank you.

J: My name's Jennifer Summers and I'm the Head of Human Resources. This is Vicky, our sales and marketing director. If you're successful, you'll be her personal assistant.

V: Hi, Charlie.

C: Hi. Nice to meet you both.

J: So, Charlie, tell us a bit about yourself.

C: Right, well I studied English Literature at university and then I started working in an office. I really like it because I enjoy working in a team and I'm good with computers.

J: So why do you want to leave your job?

C: Unfortunately, the job is only temporary. I want to work somewhere I can use my skills and have more responsibility.

J: Why do you think *you* are the right person for this job?

C: I'm very organised. I have good communication skills and I can write well – at university I worked on the student newspaper, so I have a lot of writing experience.

V: Good. As the director, my time is very important, so I need someone who can plan carefully and work quickly. How fast can you type?

C: Seventy-five words a minute.

V: That's fine. Now, do you have any experience working as a PA?

V = Vicky   C = Charlie   J = Jennifer

V: That's fine. Now, do you have any experience working as a PA?

C: No ... not working as a PA. However, I do have experience of working in an office. I'm a fast learner and I enjoy hard work.

V: This isn't an easy job and the hours are long.

C: Oh, I don't mind working long hours and I like hard work.

J: Thank you, Charlie. Do you have any questions for us?

C: Yes, can you describe a typical day?

J: The day usually starts at eight thirty, but some days you will need to come in early. First, you check emails and phone messages. Vicky needs you to remind her about her meetings when she arrives at nine o'clock. Meetings usually take place in the afternoon.

V: It's important that you have tea, coffee and biscuits ready for the meeting. You'll meet the clients in reception, so you need to be there early.

C: Yes. Definitely.

J: You take notes during the meeting. Later, you type the notes and email them to everyone. You'll also book travel for Vicky and organise her diary for her.

C: It all sounds great!

P = Presenter   J = Jovan

P: Good morning. You're listening to Terry Talk, with me, Terry Jackson. Today, I'm talking to Jovan Kubin. Jovan, welcome!

J: Thank you, Terry. I'm happy to be here.

P: Jovan, you did a study recently about happiness.

J: Yes, we wanted to find out which countries have the happiest people.

P: Interesting. How did you do this study?

J: We asked people from different countries questions about their life, their country and how happy they feel. We studied the results and made a list of countries. We put the countries in order from the happiest country to the least happy country. There are more than 20 countries on the list, but I'll tell you now about the top five happiest countries.

P: Great!

J: In fifth place, we have Australia.

P: Australia, yes.

J: Australia has great weather and most people live in nice houses or flats. Many Australians like their government and enjoy the beauty of the country. Eighty-five percent said they were happy to live in their country. In fourth place, is Sweden. Sweden has very little pollution. The air is clean and the streets are not dirty. Sweden's schools are very good and it's a safe place to have a family. Eighty-nine percent said they were happy.

P: Sounds good. What about the top three countries?

J: It probably won't surprise you that Switzerland is number three.

P: Ah, yes.

J: Swiss people are very healthy. They eat good food and go skiing on beautiful mountains. Ninety percent said they were happy. In second place is Norway. Norway is a great place to live because seventy-five percent of Norwegians have a job. Most jobs pay well, so they can live a good life, but it can be an expensive place for tourists to visit. Ninety-three percent said they were happy living in Norway.

P: OK, now for the big question. Which country is number one?

J: Well, ninety-six percent said they were happy living in Canada. This is a very high score. The main reason why people are happy in Canada is because they feel safe. Crime is very low. Other reasons are because there is good education and health care.

P: So, there you are! If you want to live a happy life, go to Canada!

J: Yes, exactly!

P: Thank you very much for joining me in the studio today, Jovan. Next up is …

UNIT 7   Recording 1

H = Helen   T = Tony   E = Elisabeth   W = Woman   M = Man

H: Good evening, everyone. Thank you for coming to this meeting to decide our plans for the new graffiti art project for our town. Local artist, Tony Dash, is here to tell us about the project.

T: Thanks, Helen. Many cities around the world have graffiti art projects. You can find them in Stockholm, Lisbon and Berlin. Lots of people visit these cities to come and look at the graffiti in the streets. I think we should do the same thing in our town.

H: Great! Many thanks, Tony. Now let's hear from someone who has lived in our town for all of her life, Elisabeth Towning.

E: I don't like this idea. Graffiti isn't art. Francis Bacon is art! There is no place for graffiti in this beautiful old town.

H: Thanks for letting us know what you think, Elisabeth. What do you say to that, Tony?

T: I'd like to say that graffiti *is* art. It's just a different kind of art from pictures you'll see in an art gallery. There are a lot of art students at the college here. We can ask them to do the graffiti art for this project. I believe that they can create some really interesting art – graffiti – for our town's streets.

E: But I'm worried that graffiti will make our town look very different. It won't look so beautiful anymore. Tourists who come here every summer won't want to visit it anymore.

T: I disagree – look at other towns. It's great for tourism there. People *do* go to visit places with graffiti. It should make *more* tourists come, not *fewer*!

H: Let's hear from some other people. Who would like to say something?

W: Me, please! All the buildings in this town look the same. I think this graffiti project will bring some colour to our streets.

M: Can I say something? I agree that art students can create some beautiful graffiti. But maybe other young people will do graffiti on the streets. We don't know if they can do it well … How can we stop them?

H: OK, many thanks for everything people have said. Now, let's have a vote to decide what we're going to do. Graffiti project or no graffiti project …

UNIT 8   Recording 1

S = Sam   J = Jane

S: Why have you got that big map? Don't you use a map app to find new places?

J: Well, no, I don't. I had a bad experience with a map app. So, never again!

S: Oh really? What happened?

J: Do you remember when I was travelling around Borneo with my sister?

S: Oh yes! I saw all your photos online. It looked amazing!

J: Well, yes, it was. But we didn't have a good time when we drove from Sabah to Brunei. My sister had a new map app for her phone. I think it was called *Find it 'n' Follow it*. It should be quite simple to use – you listen to the instructions and drive at the same time. Well, that was the plan.

S: Sounds like a good plan to me!

J: Yes, but it wasn't! We put the destination into the app, and then we set off. Everything was fine for the first hour. The map app told us to go straight on along the motorway, so that's what we did. Then it told us to take the next left at the roundabout. That's when everything started to go wrong.

S: Oh, why? What did you find after the roundabout?

J: We were in the jungle, but the road was OK, so we carried on driving. Then the map app gave a lot of directions quickly. It said we should take the next right, go past the petrol station, take the third on the left, and so on.

S: Oh dear! Were the directions too quick?

J: No, no! The problem was that there was no right or left turn, no petrol station and no other roads! There was only jungle and nothing else. The road got smaller and smaller and the trees got bigger and bigger!

S: Oh no! What did you do?

J: Well, you know my sister! She believes that technology is always right, so she wanted to continue. We drove deeper into the jungle, and the map app continued to give us false directions. Then the road stopped.

S: What? What do you mean it stopped?

J: Suddenly there was no more road. There was only jungle. And it was getting dark! Finally, my sister said that the map app must be wrong. We turned around and drove back to our starting point.

S: It sounds like a terrible experience! I understand now why you don't like map apps!

P = Presenter   J = Janet

P: Good evening. Tonight, we are talking with Janet Clarke, a TV and film expert. Welcome, Janet.

J: Thank you.

P: Janet, maybe you could start by telling us about your job.

J: You might think I just watch films and TV all day, but that's not what I do!

P: Haha.

J: No, my job is to look at numbers and information.

P: What kind of information?

J: We look at how people watch TV and movies. We try to understand *how* people watch them, and for *how long* they watch them. Then we decide what we think people are going to do in the future, and then we help companies use this information.

P: And what do you think people are going to do in the future?

J: The numbers show that the world's TV and cinema habits have changed a lot during the last few years. We think that this change will continue. Live TV and cinema are dying.

P = Presenter   J = Janet

P: Dying? Really? That sounds serious!

J: Yes. Let me explain. When I was young, we watched programmes on TV channels which had lots of adverts.

P: But we still watch these TV channels, don't we?

J: Maybe you and I do, yes. But did you know that over 40 percent of adults under 40 don't watch programmes when they are shown on TV channels!

P: Really?

J: Yes, it's true. They do watch programmes, but they don't watch them on TV channels. It's not the programmes which aren't popular, it's live TV. Young people like to choose when they watch their favourite programmes. They use apps, mobile phones and TV services like Netflix, or they watch the programmes on the internet. This different way of watching programmes has changed everything.

P: How exactly?

J: Well, look at cinema, for example. Many young people don't go to the cinema anymore. They prefer to watch films at home. They also really enjoy watching TV series, like *Game of Thrones.* Because of this, companies are making fewer films and more TV series. As a result, cinema ticket sales have gone down. The same thing happened to DVD rentals. Young people didn't need to go to a shop to rent a DVD. With online TV, they can watch anything immediately!

P: Right!

J: It's the same for live TV – if young people don't turn on their TV, they don't see adverts. If they don't see adverts, companies won't pay for advertising on TV. TV companies are worried.

P: So, what advice do you give to businesses?

J: It's simple. If young people are using apps to watch TV programmes, we need to find a way to advertise in the apps.

P: Right …

P = Presenter   M = Marsha   C1 = Caller 1   C2 = Caller 2

P: Welcome to our weekly programme, *The Dilemma Den.* Today's topic is money, but the problem isn't one that most people have. To explain, I'll introduce today's guest who has the dilemma, Marsha. Marsha, please explain your problem for our listeners.

M: Thank you! So, my problem … my dilemma … is a little unusual. I've won a very large amount of money and I don't want any of it. Well, maybe some money for my house, but I want to give most of it away. My dilemma is who do I give the money to? My family have many ideas and I'm confused!

P: Well, here's the dilemma, listeners. Marsha has no idea who to *give* … yes, you heard correctly … give her money to. Let's see if we can help her. We've got our first caller on Line 1. Hello, Line 1, what do you think?

C1:   Oh hello! Well, Marsha, I'm confused, too! Give the money to your family, of course! It's simple!

M: Can I answer this? No, I can't give the money to my family. There are too many people in my family. I don't want them to fight or become too interested in money, you know, just thinking about money and nothing else!

P: Right, I see your point there, Marsha. Let's take another call. Line 2, what do you have to say?

C2:   Morning, Marsha. I think you should find out about charities in your local area. There are so many groups with people doing good work in UK cities and towns, and they always need money because they do their work for free.

P: Thank you, caller. We've had a lot of people emailing with the same idea, to give money to charity! Here's an email suggesting that the Berkshire Bird Society needs some money. Marsha, what do you think?

M: Well, I'm not sure about giving money to birds, but I do like the idea of helping charity groups in my local area. I've lived there all my life, so this could be a chance for me to give something back.

P: That's great! *The Dilemma Den* has solved another problem! Marsha, do tell us what you do, and listeners, join us again at the same time next week for another problem in *The Dilemma Den.*

ANSWER KEY

UNIT 1

1A

1
1 what 2 where 3 which 4 why 5 whose 6 when
7 how/who

2
1 What 2 How 3 How 4 Which 5 How 6 Who
7 Where 8 When 9 Whose 10 How

3
1 c 2 a 3 i 4 b 5 e 6 h 7 j 8 g 9 f 10 d

4
1 is 2 are 3 are 4 do 5 is 6 do 7 is 8 do

5
1 **What is your** favourite food?
2 How many hours **do** you spend online?
3 **Do** you like reading?
4 Where **do** you go at weekends?
5 **Do** you talk to your friends online?
6 Where **is** your favourite restaurant?
7 Where are you **from**?
8 What **is** your favourite book?
9 **Do** you live in a city?
10 **Are** you interested in sports?

6
1 is your 2 Can you 3 do you 4 are you 5 does it

1B

1
1 ask 2 listen 3 take 4 start 5 have 6 try
7 plan 8 take

2
1 Listen 2 have 3 plan 4 again 5 care 6 off
7 try 8 ask

3
1 once 2 always 3 all 4 every 5 rarely 6 often
7 week 8 hardly

4
1 I'm always on time.
2 I often work late on Fridays.
3 He's usually tired after class.
4 I never go running at night.
5 She doesn't usually check her emails at weekends.
6 I go there all the time.
7 I rarely have time to relax.
8 I hardly ever go to the cinema.

5
1 usually have a lot of work to do
2 rarely bored
3 always make me happy
4 a team meeting once a week
5 every month
6 never have enough sleep
7 often work late

1C

1
1 a 'm studying b study
2 a try b 'm trying
3 a 'm taking b usually take
4 a use b 'm using
5 a 'm talking b talk
6 a cook b 'm cooking

2
1 ✗ I usually wake 2 ✓ 3 ✗ I'm cooking 4 ✓ 5 ✓
6 ✗ I'm living 7 ✗ She's trying

3
1 are you crying 2 do you do 3 I'm working 4 he's visiting
5 She drives 6 are you cooking 7 I'm trying

4
1 family 2 cards 3 the answers 4 money 5 social media
6 email 7 a language course 8 school

5
1 have a shower 2 start work 3 take a break 4 have lunch
5 spend time with family 6 watch a film

1D

1
1 help, need 2 clear, repeat 3 need, get 4 one, this

2
1 Which 2 Can 3 What 4 Is 5 to 6 Can 7 Did 8 It's

3
1 d 2 g 3 b 4 f 5 h 6 c 7 a 8 e

Listening

1
b

2
a 3 b 1 c 4 d 2

3a/b
1 T … *so many ways to say hello and goodbye in English-speaking countries.*
2 T *That's quite different from a normal hi and bye …*
3 F *… to say goodbye, it's 'Cheerio' …*
4 T *To say goodbye, they might say 'Take it easy' …*
5 F *In the US … people might say 'Hey! What's up?' …*
6 T *They leave with no goodbye!*
7 T *In Scotland … to say goodbye, you can say 'See you after' …*
8 F *… Scottish greetings are my favourite.*

4
1 e 2 c 3 a 4 b 5 d

Reading

1

c

2

1 F *... I'm going to live a day in her life ...*
2 F *Valerie is 108 years old ...*
3 T *... eat two raw eggs ...*
4 F *After lunch, it's time for a nap.*
5 T *For 70 years, Valerie has eaten the same for lunch ...*
6 T *... we make a simple dinner ...*
7 F *... each evening she always writes down her thoughts and feelings ...*
8 F *Why not try them?*

3

1 the same 2 always 3 easy 4 early 5 happy 6 rarely
7 never 8 always 9 Every day

4

1 boiled 2 nap 3 raw 4 unusual 5 diary 6 secret

Writing

1

b

2

1 evening 2 difficult 3 writes 4 chair 5 likes
6 doesn't help 7 takes 8 exercise

3

1 That's why 2 so that 3 so that 4 because 5 because of
6 That's why

4

Student's own answers.

5

Student's own answers.

UNIT 2

2A

1

1 happy 2 afraid 3 nervous 4 stressed 5 excited
6 angry 7 bored 8 relaxed 9 worried 10 surprised

2

1 angry, happy 2 worried, relaxed 3 bored, stressed
4 excited, nervous 5 bored, surprised

3

1 went 2 decided 3 tried 4 showed 5 felt 6 talked
7 went 8 were 9 watched 10 was

4

1 walked 2 cried 3 were 4 had 5 wrote 6 flew 7 saw
8 was

5

1 decided 2 were 3 arrived 4 talked 5 looked 6 tried
7 showed 8 flew 9 was 10 felt 11 watched 12 visited

2B

1

1 in 2 last 3 When 4 ago 5 on 5 until

2

1 d 2 b 3 f 4 a 5 c 6 e

3

1 when 2 ago 3 in 4 Last 5 until 6 on 7 on 8 ago

4

1 didn't 2 weren't 3 was 4 didn't 5 wasn't 6 didn't
7 wasn't 8 did

5

1 was 2 went 3 didn't have 4 had 5 tried 6 were
7 didn't find 8 fell over 9 ate 10 laughed

6

1 When did Jim arrive this morning?
2 Where did you buy your bike?
3 Who was at Shona's party?
4 Where did you go on holiday?
5 Why was Billy late this morning?
6 What time did they finish work?
7 Why did she travel to Italy?
8 Which film did you see at the cinema?

2C

1

1 sour 2 creamy/fresh/light 3 fresh 4 dry/plain
5 light/fresh 6 plain/dry 7 hot 8 sweet 9 delicious

2

1 hot 2 sweet 3 light 4 delicious 5 plain
6 dry 7 fresh 8 creamy 9 sour

3

1 b 2 e 3 a 4 d 5 g 6 f 7 h 8 c

4

1 some 2 a lot of 3 some 4 lots of 5 a 6 a few
7 some 8 some 9 a few 10 a little 11 a lot 12 a few
13 a 14 some

5

1 bit 2 little 3 some 4 of 5 a lot 6 a 7 any 8 an

2D

1

1 That's 2 Guess 3 exciting 4 where 5 sounds 6 lovely
7 way 8 next

2

1 b 2 a 3 f 4 c 5 d 6 e

3

1 where 2 How 3 Who 4 No way 5 How 6 sounds
7 What 8 That's

Listening

1

1 B 2 A 3 C

2

1 F *You can hold a pasty in your hand and eat it.*
2 T *They are really tasty to eat, especially on a cold day.*
3 F *You can buy them in supermarkets and in bakeries, and some pubs serve them.*
4 F *My mum made it for me when I was a child.*
5 F *It's made with food left from last night's dinner.*
6 T *It's called bubble and squeak because it makes a strange sound when you cook it.*
7 T *... the first Eccles cake was made there around 300 years ago ...*
8 F *Inside the cake there are lots of different types of fruit, usually bits of orange, lemon and currants.*

3a/b

1 b **2** c **3** c **4** a **5** b **6** c **7** c **8** a

Reading

1

1 Greece **2** Hawaii **3** West Africa **4** Spain

2

1 weren't **2** read **3** Men **4** chanted **5** has **6** has to
7 used **8** A lot of

3

1 To learn lessons from other people's mistakes.
2 Aesop.
3 Dark green.
4 They told the history of the Hawaiian people.
5 Tells the story of the village.
6 Because a griot has to learn a lot of information.
7 On the walls.
8 60,000 years ago.

4

1 special **2** cave **3** ancient **4** similar **5** mistakes

Writing

1

a

2

a 8 **b** 10 **c** 6 **d** 5 **e** 9 **f** 7 **g** 2 **h** 4 **i** 3 **j** 1

3a

well, early, carefully, calmly, quickly, angrily, fast, slowly, loudly

3b

1 carefully **2** badly **3** quickly **4** happily **5** quietly
6 easily **7** slowly **8** well

4a/b

Student's own answers.

5

Student's own answers.

UNIT 3

3A

1

1 clean **2** interesting **3** crowded **4** cheap **5** peaceful
6 exciting

2

1 old **2** lively **3** modern **4** popular **5** beautiful **6** noisy
7 dirty **8** interesting

3

 1 It's easier to phone friends than to write emails.
 2 My sister thinks maths is more difficult than English.
 3 Driving a car is worse for the environment than riding a bike.
 4 I think working with other people is less boring than working alone.
 5 They say that the new theatre is uglier than the old theatre.
 6 The river is cleaner now than it was before.
 7 This class is not as easy as the last class.
 8 Your city has better weather than mine.
 9 Brigit doesn't run faster than her sister.
10 My mobile was less expensive than my laptop.

4

 1 noisier
 2 more beautiful, more peaceful
 3 not as big as
 4 better
 5 less safe
 6 more popular
 7 older
 8 less busy
 9 not as modern as
10 more interesting

3B

1

1 24-hour **2** sea view **3** service **4** free
5 transfer **6** included **7** double **8** tours

2

1 service **2** included **3** view **4** parking
5 star **6** out **7** organised **8** reception

3

1 most **2** the highest **3** least **4** cheapest **5** biggest
6 least **7** worst **8** furthest **9** best **10** the

4

1 the oldest **2** the highest **3** the biggest
4 The least expensive **5** The most expensive
6 the most beautiful **7** the most popular **8** The safest
9 the most peaceful

5

1 This is **the** easiest way to get to the hotel.
2 I'm having **the worst** holiday! It's so boring here.
3 The **most** interesting place I've been to is Antarctica.
4 Why did you book the **smallest** room in the hotel?
5 The **best** restaurants are in this road.
6 It's the **quietest** hotel in the city, but it's also the most boring.
7 Hostels aren't always **the** cheapest option.
8 This hotel is the **most** beautiful one on the island.

3C

1

1 learn **2** fall **3** eat **4** cook **5** go **6** share **7** rides
8 visit

2

1 fall **2** drive **3** watch **4** cook **5** go **6** break **7** learn
8 be

3a

1 watched **2** eaten **3** shared **4** fallen **5** learnt

3b

1 have **2** haven't **3** hasn't **4** has **5** haven't

3c

1 c **2** b **3** a **4** e **5** d

4

1 ever **2** have **3** ever, have **4** never, learnt **5** gave, been

5

1 've never lived **2** Has (anyone) ever eaten **3** 've been to
4 didn't have **5** Have (you) ever tried **6** 've eaten
7 've never been to **8** tried

3D

1

1 d **2** c **3** a **4** e **5** f **6** b

2
1 d **2** g **3** a **4** f **5** h **6** c **7** e **8** b

Listening

1
1 A **2** J/A **3** J/A **4** A **5** J **6** A

2
1 T *I'm really sad it's finished.*
2 T *... skiing on Ben Nevis!*
3 F *... spent two weeks ...*
4 T *I like being alone. I can practise my skiing ...*
5 F *Not really. A day pass costs £20 and you can find cheap places to stay ...*
6 T *... lots of good restaurants to eat in.*
7 T *... amazing views!*
8 F *About four and a half hours' train journey from Edinburgh.*

3a/b
1 b **2** a **3** b **4** b **5** a

Reading

1
b

2
1 F *... these days many people are starting to take their holidays in the winter months*
2 F *London in November is 5–10 °C ...*
3 T *Gozo has some of the best swimming in the Mediterranean ...*
4 F *This is a 19-kilometre street market ...*
5 T *It's easy to find cheap accommodation in Marrakech.*
6 F *Take a short bus ride ...*
7 F *A trip to Paphos is good at any time of year ...*
8 T *Have you ever been surfing? Do you like riding a bike or mountain climbing? Well, you can do all of these things in November in Paphos.*

3
1 M *... you can buy any kind of food, furniture, art and jewellery ...*
2 G *... you can enjoy a comfortable 20°C on the beautiful Island of Gozo.*
3 LP *Take a short bus ride and you can go for a good walk, and enjoy the sun and fresh air.*
4 G *This quiet and peaceful place has beautiful beaches and amazing views.*
5 P *A trip to Paphos is good at any time of year ...*
6 M *The local hotels are called riads and are much cheaper than normal hotels.*
7 LP *... enjoy the 24°C temperature.*
8 M *... the perfect weather to enjoy the world-famous Medina market.*

4
1 a **2** b **3** a **4** a **5** a

Writing

1
c

2
1 T *... organised day trip ...*
2 F *We went by train ... It only takes an hour and a half ...*
3 F *Two hours in the gardens, one hour in the Jane Austen Centre.*
4 F *Lunch is included in the trip and is served in a hotel in the centre of Bath.*
5 T *We had too much time in the gardens ...*
6 T *... there's lots of walking ... if you enjoy learning about history.*

3
a 3 **b** 1 **c** 4 **d** 2

4
Student's own answers.

5
Student's own answers.

4A

1
1 holiday **2** festival **3** have **4** have **5** celebrate **6** get
7 contact **8** go out **9** have **10** give

2
1 e **2** a **3** c **4** f **5** b **6** d

3
1 going to **2** 're going **3** want **4** to do **5** 'd like to
6 doesn't want **7** 'm going to **8** wants **9** like to **10** to be

4
1 I'm going to finish university next month.
2 I'd like to leave in an hour.
3 I'm going to see her the day after tomorrow.
4 Would you like to have dinner with me this Saturday?
5 I don't want to go out tonight.
6 Can you meet me at four o'clock tomorrow?
7 I'm going to do an English course next year.

5
1 Jack **wants** to have a dinner party next week.
2 I'd like **to** go out for a meal this Friday.
3 Tonight I**'d** like to stay home and watch a film.
4 I'm tired, so I**'m** not going to go out tonight.
5 Can you call John? He **wants** to speak to you.
6 It's your mum's birthday next week. How **are** you going to celebrate?
7 I **don't** want to get a job after university. I want to travel!
8 The party is boring and I want **to** go home.

4B

1
1 e **2** c **3** a **4** d **5** f **6** b

2
1 I **won't** go for a run today, it's really cold outside!
2 Do you need some help with your homework? I**'ll** help you!
3 It's very noisy outside – I'll **close** the window.
4 I'm hungry, I think I**'ll cook** dinner early tonight.
5 It's Jenny's birthday next week. I'll **buy** her a present.
6 I've got a lot of work to do tomorrow – I won't **stay** out late tonight.

3
1 I know! I'll leave the office soon. **2** I'll answer it.
3 I'll carry them. **4** I won't do it again. **5** I won't buy any then.
6 Don't worry, I'll bring some.

4
1 set **2** choose **3** make **4** bake **5** book **6** plan **7** send
8 remind

5
1 d **2** g **3** a **4** c **5** b **6** h **7** e **8** f

4C

1
1 do I have to **2** don't have to **3** Do I have to **4** can **5** can't
6 Do I have **7** have to **8** can

2

1 have to   2 can   3 don't have to   4 can't   5 have to   6 can

3

1 don't have to have   2 can get   3 don't have to bring
4 have to be   5 can help   6 don't have to bring

4

1 excited   2 bored   3 interested   4 worried   5 surprised
6 relaxed   7 tired

5

1 a boring   b bored
2 a exciting   b excited
3 a relaxed   b relaxing
4 a tiring   b tired
5 a surprised   b surprising
6 a worried   b worrying
7 a interesting   b interested

4D

1

1 like   2 love   3 shall   4 Let's   5 good   6 join   7 think
8 want   9 busy   10 meet   11 sure   12 can   13 sounds

2

1 to join   2 love to   3 sure   4 to meet   5 meet   6 don't
7 good   8 Let's   9 want   10 I'm   11 sounds   12 shall

Listening

1

b

2

1 F *next month*
2 F *full-day celebration*
3 T *It's the 50th birthday of our company …*
4 F *We have to find a big venue.*
5 F *Pauline hates sport, especially cricket.*
6 T *I suppose it's true that not everyone likes sport.*
7 F *Danny went to a murder mystery day last year.*
8 F *Actors do a murder mystery play.*

3a/b

1 activities   2 difficult   3 bad   4 detectives   5 guess
6 find the venue   7 book   2 plan

Reading

1

c

2

1 morning   2 stays   3 the best party this year   4 isn't   5 can

3

1 The events organiser **has** got a folder with lots of useful information.
2 Elena says that it's **impossible** to give the client what she says she wants.
3 The client arrives **late** for the meeting.
4 Two weeks **isn't** enough time to do everything the client asks for.
5 Elena **isn't** worried about the celebration.
6 The client thinks that Elena **is** a good events organiser.
7 The writer thinks that the celebration **is** going to be a success.

4

1 a night to remember   2 impossible   3 folder   4 perfect
5 venue

Writing

1

1 b   2 a   3 c

2

a 1   b 2   c 3   d 1   e 3   f 2

3

We'd/I'd love you to come, I (really) hope you can make it.

4

1 love   2 unfortunately   3 to come   4 afraid   5 have
6 be there

5

1 would/'d   2 unfortunately   3 afraid   4 time   5 make

6

Student's own answers.

7

Student's own answers.

UNIT 5

5A

1

1 creative   2 customers   3 well-paid   4 from home
5 part-time   6 communication   7 long hours   8 team

2

1 part-time, good manager, home
2 well-paid, long hours, team
3 on my own, with customers, communication skills

3

1 who   2 who   3 which   4 which   5 which   6 who
7 which   8 which   9 which   10 who

4

1 Is that the boy who helped you?
2 A cruise is a holiday which is on a ship.
3 A straw is something which you can use for drinking.
4 Roger is the player who won the trophy.
5 That's the dress which I wore to the party.
6 Stella is the person who is now the manager.

5

1 d   2 f   3 a   4 g   5 c   6 e   7 b   8 h

5B

1

1 looks like   2 look   3 looks   4 look like   5 look like   6 looks
7 looks   8 looks   9 look like   10 like

2

1 Shelley is very fit and looks like an athlete.
2 Greg keeps smiling and looks really happy.
3 What does your sister look like?
4 Everyone looked really nervous on the first day.
5 Cindy and Jo look like sisters.
6 Peter looks like his father and his grandfather.
7 Karen looks very tired and unhappy today.
8 What's Ben's new girlfriend like?

3

1 looks   2 look like   3 looks like   4 look   5 looks like
6 is … like   7 looks   8 look like   9 is like   10 is … like

4

1 blonde **2** long **3** slim **4** bald **5** dark **6** tall **7** smart
8 tattoo **9** moustache

5

1 straight **2** smart **3** tall **4** short **5** slim **6** bald **7** dark
8 casual **9** curly **10** beard

5c

1

1 ask **2** keep **3** read **4** compare **5** pay **6** return **7** in a
8 try

2

1 f **2** b **3** d **4** e **5** h **6** a **7** g **8** c

3

1 in a sale **2** pay by credit card **3** kept the receipt **4** Try it on
5 compare prices **6** ask for a discount **7** read some reviews
8 return something

4

1 b **2** a **3** b **4** a **5** a **6** b **7** b **8** b **9** a **10** b

5

  1 You should **wear** …
  2 Daphne says I shouldn't **worry** …
  3 Never **leave** a child alone …
  4 You shouldn't **tell** …
  5 I should **study** …
  6 My grandmother says, '**Always help** …'
  7 You should **go** …
  8 **Never get** in a car …
  9 Mike should **call** …
10 Always **wear** …

5d

1

1 Why **2** Let's **3** buy **4** how **5** don't **6** That's **7** go

2

1 You could try watching TV.
2 How about the Tower of London?
3 Let's go home.
4 What about steak and chips?
5 Why don't you call and ask?
6 I think I'd prefer to go to the cinema.
7 You could buy her some nice chocolates.
8 OK, that's a really good idea.

Listening

1

1 PA (personal assistant) **2** Vicky

2

1 Charlie **2** English **3** computers **4** temporary
5 responsibility **6** organised **7** communication **8** write
9 75

3

1 doesn't have **2** is happy to **3** usually **4** check emails
5 9.00 **6** after **7** food and drink **8** goes

Reading

1

b

2

1 B **2** A **3** B **4** C **5** F **6** D **7** E **8** D **9** C **10** F

3

1 a **2** a **3** b **4** a **5** a **6** b **7** a **8** b **9** b

Writing

1

A 3 **B** 1 **C** 4 **D** 2

2

1 F *You can work in the UK or in another part of the world.*
2 F *You can work for a school … You can also work for yourself …*
3 T *In some countries, they work seven days a week!*
4 T *If you enjoy being creative, then planning lessons is fun!*
5 F *You need to be organised because a teacher does a lot of
    paperwork.*
6 T *They work very hard. That's why they need so much time to relax!*

3

You can work in the UK **or** you can work in another part of the world.
A lot of teachers choose to work in another country **and** this is a
great way to see the world.
You can work for a school **and** give English classes there.
You can also work for yourself **and** teach private classes.
Some teachers work from home **and** teach their lessons online.
They usually have a lot of classes **and** they want their students to
be happy …
That's why they spend a lot of time planning their lessons.
Teachers work late **and** often at the weekends, **too**.
But if you enjoy being creative, …
You need to be organised **because** a teacher does a lot of
paperwork.
You need to check homework **and** write tests.
You have to plan lessons **and** create fun activities **so** your students
are interested.
If you teach children, you have to look after them **and also** write
reports.
You should enjoy working with people, **too**, **because** you will be
working with …
They work very hard. **That's why** they need so much time to relax!

4

1 and **2** However, **3** or **4** also **5** That's why **6** too

5

Student's own answers.

6

Student's own answers.

UNIT 6

6a

1

1 family **2** good **3** simple **4** earn **5** have **6** free
7 fit **8** well

2

1 f **2** d **3** g **4** a **5** c **6** b **7** e **8** h

3

1 … people **won't** have telephones in their houses.
2 … people will **be** healthier because of new sports technology.
3 … I don't **think** people will use paper money.
4 … I think people **will** only use public transport.
5 … people will **have** more free time.
6 … I think we'll travel more.
7 … **people** won't eat so much meat.
8 … I **don't** think people will drive to work.

4

1 won't be **2** will be **3** will get **4** will enjoy **5** will rain
6 won't stay **7** won't have

5

1 People **will work** longer hours.
2 People **won't** work in offices.
3 I think **it will** be hard to relax at the weekends.
4 It'll **be** more difficult to find a job.
5 I think people will **do** more than one job.
6 I **don't** think we'll have much free time.
7 People **won't** spend a lot of time with their families.

6B

1

1 make 2 have 3 make 4 make 5 have 6 do 7 have
8 do 9 have 10 do 11 have 12 do 13 have 14 do

2

1 i 2 f 3 e 4 a 5 g 6 b 7 c 8 j 9 d 10 h

3

1 Who are you having lunch with on Monday?
2 What are you doing on Friday evening?
3 Are you working in the office on Tuesday?
4 When are you going to the gym?
5 How many times are you doing yoga this week?
6 When are you meeting your mum for dinner?
7 Who are you going to the cinema with?
8 Are you doing anything on Thursday?

4

1 I'm having lunch with Chris on Monday.
2 I'm flying to Rome on Friday evening.
3 No, I'm travelling to Birmingham.
4 I'm going to the gym on Friday at 12.30 p.m.
5 I'm doing yoga two times/twice this week.
6 I'm meeting my mum for dinner on Wednesday evening.
7 I'm going to the cinema with Sarah.
8 No, I'm having a day off.

5

1 are (you) doing 2 're going 3 'm starting 4 'm (not) cooking
5 is leaving 6 're having 7 're playing 8 are (you) meeting

6C

1

do: activities, gardening, homework, nothing, yoga
go: dancing/clubbing, cycling, shopping, swimming
play: in a band, video games, volleyball

2

1 going 2 do 3 plays 4 go 5 nothing 6 go 7 yoga
8 video games 9 activities 10 running

3

1 You shouldn't order too much food because you **might** not finish it!
2 I didn't study very hard, so I might **not** pass the exam.
3 When I leave university, I **might** do some travelling.
4 I want to do some exercise this weekend, but I **may** not have enough time.
5 It's going to be sunny tomorrow, so I might **do** some gardening.
6 My back is hurting a lot, so I **might** go the doctor.
7 I want to see the new horror film, but my friends may **not** want to.
8 I might **have** a barbecue this weekend.

4

1 might not 2 might 3 may 4 may 5 may not 6 might
7 might not 8 may

5

1 I may/might see you later.
2 I may/might not have time to see you today.
3 It may/might not rain tomorrow.
4 John may/might not like spicy food.
5 I may/might do some cooking tonight.
6 The shop may/might be open late tomorrow.
7 It may/might not be a good idea.
8 I may/might go dancing this weekend.

6D

1

1 This is a message for Mrs Davis
2 but I have to cancel your appointment
3 Call me back on
4 I'm calling to tell you
5 back when you get this
6 this is your mother
7 I'm calling about
8 Give me a call
9 I'm calling to remind you about
10 text me when you're free / when you're free, text me

2

1 is 2 cancel 3 let 4 remind 5 call 6 calling 7 give

Listening

1

1st Canada 2nd Norway 3rd Switzerland 4th Sweden
5th Australia

2

1 weather 2 like 3 schools are 4 Ninety 5 work 6 safe

3a/b

1 Sweden 2 Norway 3 Canada 4 Switzerland 5 Australia
6 Norway 7 Sweden 8 Canada 9 Australia
10 Switzerland

Reading

1

1 e 2 c 3 d 4 a 5 b

2

1 F *These small things could change your life!*
2 T *Books help us understand the world.*
3 T *A good exercise routine also helps us to not feel stressed.*
4 F *You might think that successful people have to work all the time, but this is not true.*
5 F *Sometimes they work for free because it makes them feel happy.*
6 T *For many people, it's normal to spend a lot of time at work.*

3

1 New cultures and environments.
2 Communicate better with people around us.
3 At least three times every week.
4 We can get stronger, healthier, not feel stressed, feel good and look good.
5 Playing guitar in a band and learning how to dance.
6 They can help us feel ready to start work the next day, with new ideas.
7 They can give money to places that help poor people or they can give a job to someone who needs one.
8 It makes them feel happy.
9 We can feel sad and lonely.
10 Time with family and friends.

4

1 improve 2 regularly 3 a break 4 local community
5 lonely

Writing

1

She has too many things to do, so she feels very stressed.

2

1 At university.
2 Because her calendar is too full.
3 Because her parents came to visit her.
4 To talk about her exam results.
5 Michelle's best friend, Claire, is having a party.
6 She needs to organise her time better.

3a

1 using paragraphs 2 clearer 3 one main idea
4 introduces the topic 5 give details

4

1 I'm really busy right now
2 the last few weeks were busy, too
3 next week is the same
4 being busy can make life hard

5

Student's own answers.

6

Student's own answers.

UNIT 7

7A

1

1 area 2 cycle 3 flats 4 good 5 local 6 neighbours
7 nightlife 8 traffic

2

1 public transport 2 cycle paths 3 pollution 4 local
5 neighbours 6 area 7 location 8 flat 9 nightlife
10 traffic

3

1 enough 2 too 3 too much 4 many 5 strong enough
6 too busy 7 enough money 8 not clean enough

4

1 too many 2 too 3 too many 4 too much 5 too
6 too much 7 too many 8 too

5

1 Do you think the house is **big enough** for us?
2 Holly says there is **enough food** for the party.
3 There **isn't** enough time for us to catch the train.
4 Many cities don't have enough **big spaces**.
5 Those jeans aren't **long enough** for your legs!
6 Do we **have** enough food for everyone?

7B

1

1 mountain 2 forest 3 stream 4 river 5 ocean 6 beach
7 wood 8 hill

2

1 beach 2 ocean 3 forest 4 hill 5 stream 6 lake
7 mountain 8 sea 9 river 10 wood

3

1 used to 2 didn't use to 3 used to 4 use to
5 didn't use to 6 use to 7 used to 8 used to

4

1 As a child, I used to live near the sea.
2 Did you use to swim in the lake when you were young?
3 My brother used to have purple hair and a big beard.
4 We used to be really good friends, but now we don't speak at all.
5 Did Crystal use to work for your family?
6 The giraffes didn't use to come into the forest.
7 We used to write letters, but now we only write emails.
8 I didn't use to enjoy cooking, but now I love it.

5

1 Did you **use** to cycle to school …
2 My teachers used to **shout** at me …
3 My brother didn't use **to** eat green vegetables …
4 What did you use to **do** before …
5 I **used** to know lots of people …
6 When I was at school, we used **to** do …
7 Nick **didn't** use to enjoy …
8 Sam used to **be** less fit …

7C

1

1 b 2 a 3 c 4 b 5 b 6 c 7 c 8 a 9 c 10 b

2

1 opposite 2 next to 3 on 4 behind 5 in the middle of
6 in front of 7 between 8 in the corner 9 under

3

1 a 2 – 3 the 4 an 5 a 6 – 7 – 8 the 9 a 10 –

4

1 a, the, –, The 2 a, –, –, –, a, The, an 3 the, a, –, –

7D

1

1 I'm really sorry I'm late.
2 I'm sorry I don't have enough money.
3 I'm afraid I didn't bring my computer with me.
4 I'm busy so I can't meet you later, sorry.
5 I can't come to book club tonight, sorry.

2

a matter b problem c mind d worry e all right

3

1 d 2 a 3 e 4 c 5 b

4

1 sorry, worry 2 afraid, matter 3 can't, Never
4 really, worries

Listening

1

No.

2

1 F … the new graffiti art project for our town.
2 T You can find them in Stockholm, Lisbon and Berlin.
3 F … someone who has lived in our town for all of her life, Elisabeth Towning.
4 T There are a lot of art students at the college here …
5 F Elizabeth says there is no place for graffiti; Tony says that graffiti is art.
6 T … some really interesting art – graffiti – for our town's streets.
7 T … this graffiti project will bring some colour to our streets.
8 F Now, let's have a vote to decide what we're going to do.

3a/b

1 lives 2 doesn't like 3 isn't 4 a different kind of art from
5 can 6 fewer 7 will 8 don't know

Reading

1

b

2

1 F *I think a lot of people like the idea.*
2 T *... real life on a canal boat is very different from the idea!*
3 F *... for more than half the year, it can be cold and wet.*
4 F *... you can only travel at four miles per hour.*
5 F *You can pay to stay in one place, but this can be very
   expensive.*
6 F *Lots of companies sell boats.*
7 T *... can cost between £25,000 and £75,000.*
8 F *... your costs should be about 70–80 percent less than for a
   flat or house.*

3

1 The canals are green with trees and nature and the boats are
   colourful. Also, people feel free on a boat.
2 It can be cold and wet.
3 You can only travel at four miles per hour.
4 You have to move your boat every two weeks. This can be difficult and some people don't want to move so much.
5 You have to pay and it can be expensive.
6 You might not like boat life.
7 It can be 70–80 percent cheaper.
8 You need to be able to fix them.

4

1 quiet 2 colourful 3 beautiful 4 expensive 5 spend
6 fix

Writing

1

To ask if he and Sophie can visit him.

2

1 different countries 2 outside 3 short 4 wants 5 UK
6 doesn't live

3

Great to hear from you.
Everything's fine here.
(Sophie's new job) sounds fantastic!
Bye for now.

4

1 things 2 sounds 3 Take 4 is 5 can't 6 hear 7 Bye

5

Student's own answers.

6

Student's own answers.

UNIT 8

 8A

1

1 was sitting, came 2 was looking, saw
3 fell over, was walking 4 was eating, heard
5 saw, was shopping 6 came, was watching
7 met, was travelling 8 saw, were wearing

2

1 didn't go 2 ate 3 wasn't listening 4 was raining
5 were arguing 6 injured 7 didn't enjoy 8 was cleaning
9 didn't play 10 was travelling

3

1 a 2 last 3 once 4 while 5 ago 6 days 7 week
8 when

4

1 into 2 around 3 up 4 over 5 out 6 down 7 around
8 back

5

1 f 2 c 3 h 4 d 5 b 6 a 7 g 8 e

8B

1

1 a car 2 a flight 3 a bike 4 a train 5 a car
6 a holiday 7 a bus 8 a taxi

2

1 missed 2 rent 3 take 4 parked 5 got in 6 get out of
7 got on 8 got off

3

1 c 2 a 3 h 4 d 5 b 6 e 7 g 8 f

4

1 to 2 so 3 to 4 because 5 because 6 because 7 so
8 to

5

1 because my car broke down
2 so I wouldn't be late
3 to visit an old friend
4 because the view is beautiful
5 to buy some food for dinner
6 so I can stay healthy

8C

1

1 trying 2 sightseeing 3 tour 4 plan 5 pack 6 book
7 alone 8 cruise 9 shopping

2

1 pack 2 going on 3 booked 4 travelling 5 going 6 go

3

1 don't mind 2 would like 3 want 4 love 5 hate 6 want

4

1 to go 2 to plan 3 travelling 4 packing 5 trying 6 to go

5

1 I want to try some local food.
2 I enjoy renting a bike on holiday.
3 I don't want to travel by boat. It makes me feel sick.
4 I don't mind staying in a hostel.
5 I'd like/I would like to go to the beach tomorrow.
6 I love going on cruises.

8D

1

1 a 2 b 3 b 4 b 5 c 6 a 7 c 8 a

2

1 on, At, on, to 2 on, on, on, at 3 at, on, on 4 on, At, on, to

Listening

1

c

2

1 F *... travelling around the island of Borneo with my sister?*
2 F *... when we drove from Sabah to Brunei.*
3 T *... you listen to the instructions and drive at the same time.*
4 T *... We were in the jungle ...*
5 F *... she wanted to continue.*
6 T *...Then the road stopped.*
7 F *... it was getting dark!*
8 T *... drove back to our starting point.*

3a/b

1 b **2** a **3** b **4** a **5** c **6** a **7** b **8** b

Reading

1

c

2

1 F *... most people ...*
2 T *Teachers, bankers, waiters, young people and old people ... get to places.*
3 F *About eight million people are in the skies each day!*
4 T *... usually only very rich people could travel.*
5 F *... travel started to change during the nineteenth century ... railways and trains were built ... cars and good roads ... more people started to fly in aeroplanes.*
6 T *Most people lived near their friends and family ...*
7 F *To travel from London to Paris would take six days and many different horses.*
8 T *When they have a holiday ... travel to another country ... Lots of people ... friends and family all over the world.*

3

1 a different **2** all **3** flying **4** fewer **5** wanted **6** had
7 love **8** might

4

1 in the skies **2** a number of **3** century **4** instead of
5 available

Writing

1

1 She's in New Zealand.
2 She's using a campervan.
3 She leaving today.

2

1 visit Paradise Valley **2** swim in Lake Tekapo **3** go fishing
4 go to Mount Cook **5** watch the sun rise
6 go to the North Island **7** relax on the beach
8 visit Coromandel

3

Today, This morning, Last week, last Monday, last Wednesday,
last Friday, the day before yesterday, Tomorrow,
The day after tomorrow, next week, the week after next

4

1 Tomorrow **2** last night **3** This morning **4** Today
5 last Tuesday **6** Next week **7** Last week
8 the day after tomorrow

5

Student's own answers.

6

Student's own answers.

 9A

1

1 make **2** argue **3** keep **4** old **5** get **6** meet **7** see
8 disagrees **9** close

2

1 argue **2** text **3** close **4** disagree **5** friend, get on
6 touch **7** make **8** meet **9** see

3

1 Sue hasn't done any homework for a week.
2 They have been at the beach for two hours.
3 Dolly hasn't called me for months.
4 Roger has made lots of friends since he went to university.
5 Jim has had a dog for five years.
6 They haven't sent me a birthday card since we argued.
7 Ana has lived in Argentina for 15 years.
8 We have been close friends since we were at school.

4

1 for **2** since **3** for **4** for **5** since **6** since **7** since
8 for

5

1 've worked **2** for **3** 've been **4** since **5** Have (you) moved
6 've lived **7** since **8** 's been **9** for

9B

1

1 long **2** funny **3** boring **4** true **5** popular **6** sad
7 silly **8** scary **9** interesting

2

1 true **2** clever **3** long **4** serious **5** silly **6** sad
7 exciting **8** boring **9** scary

3

1 haven't been **2** 's (already) forgotten **3** 've (just) seen
4 have (just) eaten **5** haven't told **6** has (just) bought
7 've (already) finished **8** hasn't given

4

1 Have you been to the new café yet?
2 I have already given you the books you wanted.
3 I haven't met Ben's new girlfriend yet.
4 They have just left to go to the station.
5 Dotty has already baked the cake for the party.
6 Simon has just finished writing a new book.

5

1 just **2** yet **3** just **4** already **5** yet **6** just **7** yet
8 already **9** already

 9C

1

1 for **2** at **3** take **4** at **5** do **6** at **7** find **8** do
9 find **10** at **11** at **12** in **13** find **14** pass

2

1 f **2** b **3** d **4** a **5** e **6** c

3

1 I **find** working in a café difficult. I can't concentrate.
2 She's busy studying **for** her economics exams at university.
3 I want to **do** well in the fun run, so I run every day.
4 I **took** my English exam yesterday. I think I passed.

5 I want to be good **at** photography and then I can start my own photography business.

6 Over the years, I've got better **at** painting pictures.

4

1 c **2** c **3** b **4** a **5** b **6** a

5

1 could make **2** couldn't write **3** couldn't understand
4 couldn't remember **5** could run **6** couldn't decide
7 couldn't travel **8** couldn't stay awake

9D

1

1 of **2** know **3** I don't **4** Could **5** I'm not **6** Could
7 know **8** afraid

2

1 how **2** a **3** if **4** no **5** much **6** of **7** what **8** am

3

1 you know where the ticket office
2 you tell me how much a return ticket
3 you know if there is a toilet on the
4 you tell me what time the next train
5 you know if there is a bank near
6 you know how long the journey

Listening

1

1 isn't **2** gives companies advice **3** less

2

1 T *We still watch these TV channels, don't we? ... Maybe you and I do, yes.*
2 F *... over 40 percent of adults under 40 don't watch programmes when they are shown on TV channels!*
3 F *It's not the programmes which aren't popular, its live TV.*
4 T *They use apps ...*
5 F *Many young people don't go to the cinema anymore.*
6 T *With online TV, they can watch anything immediately!*
7 T *If they don't see adverts, companies won't pay for advertising on TV.*
8 F *TV companies are worried.*

3

1 b **2** b **3** a **4** a **5** a **6** b

Reading

1

a

2

a 5 **b** 1 **c** 2 **d** 3 **e** 7 **f** 4 **g** 6

3

1 F *This friend has a lot of life experience and can give you good advice.*
2 T *... you spend time with friends who are similar to you. This is why you get on so well.*
3 T *You can tell them all your secrets because you know you can trust them.*
4 F *They make your work life easier because they share the same problems as you.*
5 F *This friend can teach you a lot about other people and their traditions and opinions*
6 T *If everyone told the truth all the time, we might not like it! For this reason, friends sometimes lie.*
7 F *... and they are very confident*

4

1 a **2** d **3** f **4** c **5** b **6** e

Writing

1

1 b **2** a

2

1 M **2** J **3** M **4** M **5** J/M **6** M

3

Dear Sir or Madam
I am writing to apply for the position of ...
Please find attached ...
During this time ...
I am available for an interview
I look forward to hearing from you.
Yours faithfully,

4

1 I am writing to apply for the position of school counsellor.
2 Please find attached my CV.
3 During this time, I learnt about the latest research.
4 I look forward to hearing from you.
5 I am available for an interview at any time.

5

1 Dear Sir or Madam,
2 I am writing to apply for the position of
3 Please find attached my CV.
4 during this time
5 I am available for an interview at any time.
6 I look forward to hearing from you.
7 Yours faithfully,

6a/b

Student's own answers.

7

Student's own answers.

UNIT 10

10A

1

1 save, cost, waste **2** earn **3** lend, cash **4** pay for, credit
5 borrow, spend

2

1 d **2** h **3** a **4** g **5** c **6** f **7** b **8** e

3

1 like, 'll love **2** 'll call, have **3** passes, 'll go **4** won't, don't
5 are, 'll need **6** 'll have, is **7** 'll waste, buy **8** don't, won't

4

1 If you only buy what you need, you'll save money.
2 You shouldn't buy expensive things if you want to save money.
3 If you use special offers from newspapers and magazines, you'll spend less.
4 You'll find more discounts if you shop in the evening,
5 If you use a shopping app, it will help save you money.
6 You can find better prices if you visit more than one supermarket.

5

1 can **2** don't **3** want **4** if **5** you **6** will **7** won't
8 shouldn't

10B

1

1 was discovered **2** was called **3** ate **4** grows **5** is made
6 drink **7** are used **8** spend

2

1 was invented   **2** are used   **3** was sold   **4** have   **5** are sent
6 was flown   **7** are bought   **8** made

3

1 wasn't invented by one person
2 was worked on by many people
3 was chosen by Jaron Lanier in 1987
4 virtual reality was used for computer games
5 are enjoyed by both kids and adults these days
6 is used by the US army
7 are helped by doctors using virtual reality
8 than $15 billion dollars was spent on virtual reality last year

4

1 ago   **2** these   **3** For a long time   **4** until   **5** during   **6** Each
7 century   **8** nowadays   **9** During   **10** three days ago

5

1 I hate it when people talk **during** the film.
2 I won't finish work **until** six thirty this evening!
3 We don't see each other much **these** days.
4 The first film was made in the late 19th **century**.
5 A few years **ago**, I went to China for the first time.
6 You're late! I've been waiting **for** 45 minutes!
7 I love you more **each** day.
8 **Nowadays**, almost everyone has a mobile phone/Almost everyone has a mobile phone **nowadays**.

 10c

1

1 always had   **2** was   **3** wasn't working   **4** spent   **5** loved
6 was working   **7** was doing   **8** had

2

1 is   **2** 've (never) had   **3** 've (finally) found   **4** want
5 haven't found   **6** 're looking for   **7** need   **8** 've enjoyed
9 am (I) looking for

3

1 won't be   **2** will take   **3** Are you going to have   **4** are doing
5 will spend   **6** will enjoy   **7** won't be   **8** are going to do

4

1 My friends are coming to my house tonight.
2 I think it'll rain tomorrow.
3 I was playing volleyball when I fell over.
4 On Fridays I usually eat in a restaurant.
5 The baby's sleeping now.
6 Next year I'm going to change jobs.
7 I went to the shops yesterday.
8 I've lived here all my life.

5

1 of   **2** fun   **3** about   **4** new   **5** find   **6** up   **7** join   **8** time

6

1 tries   **2** given   **3** doing   **4** join   **5** made   **6** be
7 learning   **8** spend

10d

1

1 got   **2** Can   **3** What's   **4** mean   **5** see   **6** mean   **7** I don't

2

1 What's a sleeper?   **2** What was that last part again?
3 I'm not sure what you mean.   **4** I see.
5 What do you mean exactly?   **6** Can you say that again?
7 I still don't understand.   **8** Oh, got it!

Listening

1
b

2
1 F   *... the problem isn't one that most people have.*
2 T   *... maybe some money for my house ...*
3 T   *My dilemma is who do I give the money to?*
4 F   *There are too many people in my family.*
5 F   *I don't want them to ... become too interested in money ...*
6 T   *... the same idea, to give money to charity!*
7 F   *... I do like the idea ...*
8 T   The Dilemma Den *has solved another problem!*

3a/b
1 b   **2** c   **3** a   **4** c   **5** b   **6** a   **7** b   **8** b

Reading

1
b

2
a 3   **b** 5   **c** 1   **d** 4   **e** 2

3
1 some   **2** can   **3** a child   **4** an exciting   **5** didn't know
6 not very   **7** in her home town   **8** should

4
1 valuable   **2** hidden   **3** huge   **4** forgotten   **5** attics
6 owned

Writing

1
To help her family and friends buy the right presents.

2
1 In six weeks.
2 Yes, she has a clear idea about the watch she wants.
3 Because she goes to work after the gym.
4 Because her sunglasses are old.
5 She wants white trainers.

3

size	small, wide, big
age	old, new
shape	square, round
colour	brown, black, yellow, green, white
material	leather, gold, cotton, plastic, metal

4
1 I've lost my big, silver earrings.
2 I found a pair of old, blue, cotton trousers.
3 My mum made a big, round, pink cake.
4 I left my new, red, plastic pencil case in the classroom.
5 I bought a big, square, leather sofa.
6 Have you got my old, blue, denim shorts?

5a/b
Student's own answers.

6
Student's own answers.